THE INSIDER RAIL GUID

# Inverness to Kyle of

CW00383669

David Spaven and David Fasken

KESSOCK BOOKS

First published in Great Britain by Kessock Books 2017
Copyright © David Spaven and David Fasken 2017

A CIP catalogue record for this book is available from the British Library

ISBN 978-0-9930296-8-4

Cover design by Audiografix
Text design and typesetting by Stanford DTP
Printed and bound in Great Britain by CPI Group (UK), Croydon, CR40 4YY

# Contents

# Acknowledgements

As well as our own knowledge of the railway, gathered over more than 50 years – and my research for *Highland Survivor: the story of the Far North Line* – this guide has benefited enormously from the detailed research and writing of a variety of authors, notably David McConnell, *Rails to Kyle of Lochalsh* (1997); Michael Pearson, *Iron Roads to the Far North & Kyle* (2003); Peter Tatlow, *The Dingwall & Skye Railway* (2016); John Thomas, *The Skye Railway* (1990); and HA Vallance, *The Highland Railway* (1963). *The Dingwall & Skye Railway* is not only an absorbing read. It is also copiously illustrated, and we are particularly grateful to Peter Tatlow for permission to reproduce seven photographs from his book. All photographers, over and above shots from our own collections, are credited in the relevant photo captions. Special mention here should go to Richard Casserley and Bill Roberton for their contributions.

This is the fifth of my books to have benefited from Alan Young's splendid hand-drawn maps, which are fittingly complemented by renowned Inverness-based artist Merrill MacWilliam's evocative sketches. The text is largely my work, but David Fasken also offered many insights on the road to final publication. We also travelled the line again in Spring 2017 to bring our observations fully up to date, and then supplemented the rail experience with a trip by car to capture on camera some of the glorious landscapes where today's railway is an unobtrusive but essential part of the scenery. This book has been very much a team effort.

*David Spaven, Edinburgh, June 2017*

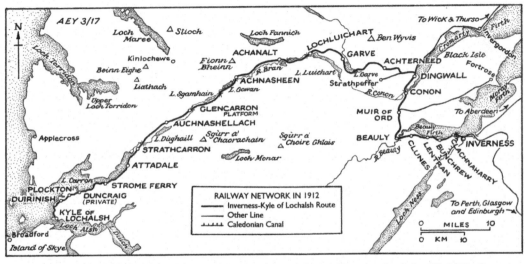

Alan Young's hand-drawn map shows the peacetime heyday of the Kyle line and branches, just before World War One. Interestingly, 'Auchnashellach' was spelt as such in the *Bradshaw* timetable of summer 1887, changing to 'Achnashellach' in the *Bradshaw* of winter 1895, and back to 'Auchnashellach' in the *Bradshaw* of April 1910, subsequently reverting for a final time to today's spelling. *Alan Young*

# Introduction

To travel by train from Inverness to Kyle of Lochalsh is to experience one of the most dramatic railway journeys in Europe.

Linking the North Sea and Atlantic coasts, the 'Dingwall & Skye Railway' forms the western leg of Britain's most northerly cross-country rail route: from Aberdeen in the east to Kyle of Lochalsh in the west.

The Inverness to Kyle railway – built in three stages between 1860 and 1897 – was created to open up a hitherto remote and inaccessible country to economic development, but the Victorians were also quick to acknowledge its outstanding scenic qualities. Much has been written about its construction, engineering features, locomotives and train services – and the three major threats to its existence in the late 20th century, all of which the railway survived.

The story of the Kyle line is inextricably linked to tourism. Unsurprisingly, many tourist guides to the route – from simple brochures to lavish colour booklets – have been produced over the years. However, unlike some of these guides, this new *Insider Rail Guide* series presents an entertaining, informative and practical guide to your rail journey.

We won't distract you with technical details but we will draw your attention to all kinds of useful insights into the history of today's railway, its distinctive architecture and operational quirks, how best to plan your journey and, above all, how to appreciate fully the view from your carriage window.

Unlike so much tourist literature, we won't assume that the sun is shining gloriously throughout your journey. This is a wise precaution, given that the English translation of the Gaelic placename 'Achnasheen' (the watershed between the east and west coasts) is 'field of rain'. Rather, we will encourage you to see the beauty of the landscape in all kinds of weather.

Nor will we pretend that the trains always run on time (although they usually do) but we'll equip you with enough insights to understand what's going on if running late, and how best to appreciate the natural and man-made surroundings if your westbound train is standing at a lonely 'crossing loop' (where trains cross on the otherwise single-track line) while patiently awaiting its eastbound counterpart. The *Insider Rail Guides* series is written by two authors steeped in Highland railways. David Spaven and David Fasken moved their respective homes from Edinburgh to Inverness as schoolboys.

Their fathers had joined the then newly established Highlands and Islands Development Board based in the town, and in 1966 these schoolboys discovered a shared enthusiasm for 'the railway', which would take them on many occasions by train to Dingwall and points west. Both became campaigners against the 1972–74 threat of closure of the Kyle line. David Spaven then began, on the Inverness-Wick/Thurso 'Far North Line', a working life in and around the rail industry, while David Fasken has over the years been an inveterate Highland rail traveller. Both authors have written several books over the last few years: notably David Spaven's *The Railway Atlas of Scotland* and *Highland Survivor: the story of the Far North Line*, and David Fasken's *Light Hearted Lines*, recounting tales of rail travel and railway life in and around Inverness in the late 1960s and early 1970s.

Join them in the following pages in a unique exploration of one of the outstanding routes on Scotland's rail network: the line from Inverness to Kyle of Lochalsh.

# CHAPTER ONE
# A history of the line

## Before the railway

In the first half of the 19th century, the extensive territory of the Highland mainland – Ross-shire, Sutherland and Caithness – to the north of the region's largest town, Inverness, was still experiencing the fundamental economic and social changes which had been imposed by the British state in the aftermath of the 1745 Jacobite Rebellion.

Subsistence farming in the Highlands had for centuries been based on 'transhumance', the practice of moving livestock, overwhelmingly cattle, from one grazing ground to another in a seasonal cycle. In winter, the cattle remained on low-lying land where arable crops would be cultivated in summer in strips or rigs ('run rigs'), and in summer the animals were moved to higher-lying 'shielings'.

However, many landowners (a combination of several Highland clan chiefs, other local landed gentry and an increasing number of southern incomers) were seeking to realise greater profit from their holdings through large-scale sheep farming. The combination of land 'improvement', the elimination of transhumance and the frequently enforced, and often brutal, clearance of much of the native population from the land (to coastal villages, or abroad, generally to North America) permitted widespread exploitation of the new cash crop, wool, and brought unprecedented prosperity to landowners. The landowners (or 'lairds') wished to fund their increasingly extravagant London lifestyles, and so learned to loosen the bonds of clan kinship and replace them with a 'rentier' attitude.

Communication within the region had traditionally been by horse tracks, 'drove roads' for cattle, or sea. The first metalled roads were built by the military following the Jacobite Rebellion of 1715, almost all of these roads being located to the south and east of Inverness.

*Bradshaw's Descriptive Railway Handbook* for 1863 described the humble earlier circumstances of Inverness:

> [it] lies as it were at the back of Scotland, in a part formerly little visited or accessible. About the year 1770, it had no banks, lamps or tiled houses, and one cargo of coals (called "blackstones") a year was enough to supply the demand; but smuggled tea, brandy, fish and game were plentiful.

By the end of the 18th century, when the possibility of a further Jacobite rebellion had receded, the maintenance of the military roads was handed over to civilian labour. The roads' subsequent rapid deterioration led, in 1803, to the establishment of the Commission for Roads and Bridges in the Highlands. The Caledonian Canal Commission was established the same year to build a waterway linking the east and west coasts through Lochs Ness, Oich and Lochy. The engineer for both Commissions was Thomas Telford, one of Britain's leading civil engineers.

A classic pre-World War One scene at the northern platforms of Inverness station, epitomising simple cross-platform connection. On the left, the overnight train from the south sits at Platform 6, having traversed the Rose Street Curve and reversed back into the station. Meanwhile, on the right, a Highland Railway train for the north waits to depart from Platform 7. *WDG Chalmers collection, courtesy of Peter Tatlow*

Despite significant improvements in communications in the first decades of the 19th century, the region still lagged far behind the level of economic development being experienced in Central Scotland. HA Vallance records in *The Highland Railway* (1963):

In the years following the Industrial Revolution, when many parts of the country were experiencing a trade boom, with its consequent increase of wealth, the Highlands of Scotland were plunged in the depths of financial depression, and poverty was rife... The absence of mineral wealth retarded, to a great extent, the development of the country; but the chief obstacle was the lack of good transport, which prevented such industries as did exist from securing a wide market and a ready outlet for their wares.

## The first Highland railways

The physical barrier of the Grampian Mountains checked the direct advance of the rail network northwards to the Highlands. However, a train journey from the Central Belt to Inverness, albeit a circuitous one via lower-lying country along the east coast, first became possible in 1858 when the Inverness & Aberdeen Junction Railway completed its final link from Nairn to Keith (which the Great North of Scotland Railway's line from Aberdeen had reached in 1856). This followed the opening in 1855 of the first railway in the Highlands: from Inverness to Nairn.

Garve station building seen looking east from the rear of a westbound train on 21 July 1931. The unusually wide 'six foot' between the two tracks – designed for the passage of fishing boats by rail (an abortive project) – is clearly evident. Note also the four hand-barrows for parcels and mail. The building contained the station office, within which on the ground floor were the booking hall and the waiting room. The first floor housed the stationmaster's accommodation. *HC Casserley*

Soon after the Inverness & Nairn Railway opened, the attention of prospective railway promoters turned to the possibility of an extension northwards from Inverness. There was initial uncertainty about the best route, with one scheme proposing to establish a steamer service between Nairn and the north shore of the Cromarty Firth, then connecting with onward rail services. The reason for the uncertainty was the perceived heavy expense of an Inverness-Dingwall railway bridging the River Ness, the Caledonian Canal, and the Rivers Beauly and Conon.

In 1859, Murdoch Paterson, who had been assistant to Joseph Mitchell on the construction of the railway from Inverness to Nairn and onward to Keith, undertook, together with his brother William Paterson and Mitchell, a survey of the landward route from Inverness to Invergordon via Beauly and Dingwall. The Inverness & Ross-shire Railway Act was then passed unopposed at Westminster in 1860, and the directors, who were primarily local and regional landowners led by Alexander Matheson of Ardross, raised sufficient capital to meet the estimated cost of £215,000 for 31 miles of single-track railway (there being insufficient population and industry to justify double-track).

On 19 September 1860, the first sod was cut in Inverness by Lady Matheson. David Ross in *The Highland Railway* (2010) described an appropriately festive occasion on a day which was observed as a general holiday in the town:

A public gathering in the Academy Park in Inverness, and a procession through the town, marked the start of work. The navvies were entertained to beef, bread and ale in "a specially erected booth",

A number of railway buildings served Achnasheen, seen looking east from a westbound train on 18 June 1937: starting at the far end are the goods shed, signal box, Station Hotel, station building, parcels bothy and toilet block. *HC Casserley*

while the quality went to the Station Hotel for a lunch that lasted from 1 p.m. to shortly after 10 p.m.

The construction of the railway was pushed forward rapidly by Scottish 'navvies' (a word derived from the 'navigators' who built the first 'navigation canals' in the 18th century), unlike many lines further south where Irish labour dominated.

## Rails reach Ross-shire

The section of railway from Inverness to the burgh of Dingwall was opened in June 1862, thus fulfilling the prediction of the 16th/17th-century Brahan Seer about 'long strings of carriages without horses' running between Dingwall and Inverness. David Ross relates that, at a celebratory lunch in Dingwall two days after the opening, Provost Falconer:

described the arrival of the railway as "…beyond all comparison the most momentous event that has ever occurred in its annals since the title of 'royal' was conferred upon it by Alexander 1 in 1226". Inverness to Dingwall by coach (inside rate) had been 7s 6d; now by train the first class return was 4s 6d, and a third class return only 1s 6½d.

Locomotive No. 17956 shunting Achnashellach while working the 4.05 train from Inverness on 18 June 1937. The loco is returning from the goods siding (*to the left*) to pick up wagons attached to the rear of the train, as required by 1891 Board of Trade regulations , and eventually complied with by the Highland Railway in 1897. *HC Casserley*

When the Inverness & Ross-shire Railway reached Dingwall in 1862, followed by various extensions which took the Far North Line through to Wick and Thurso by 1874, attention then turned to the economic opportunities which could be realised by a rail route through to the west coast. This held out the prospect of sending livestock south without the loss of meat quality from 'droving' through the mountains and, in particular, opening up the western fishing grounds for the first time to the London market. As HA Vallance writes in *The Highland Railway*:

> Because of the mountainous configuration of the country, there are only certain routes along which a crossing from east to west can be made. From very early times, these passes through the hills have been used for roads, and any railway crossing the country must of necessity follow approximately the same route. One of these natural highways runs westwards from Dingwall, the county town of Ross-shire, up Strath Conon and Strath Bran. Thence it passes over the watershed into Strath Carron. The coast is reached at a point opposite the Isle of Skye, on the sheltered waters of the Inner Sound. The distance from sea to sea is a little over 60 miles. The western end of this road forms a convenient port for the Isle of Skye and the Outer Hebrides.

In 1865 powers were granted by Parliament for the construction of the 64-mile Dingwall & Skye Railway, from Dingwall via the spa village of Strathpeffer and Straths Bran and Carron to the west coast village of Kyle of Lochalsh, on the sheltered waters of the Inner Sound immediately opposite

'In a busy scene at Dingwall, probably in 1938 or 1939, the train for Kyle of Lochalsh waits for custom. Ladies, gentlemen, children and prams are ready to board the train, or to greet friends who have just arrived. A two-wheeled handcart is positioned beside an electric light pole, while a horse and dray loaded with goods stands on the platform with the carter in attendance; behind is the refreshment room.' Peter Tatlow in *The Dingwall & Skye Railway. Peter Tatlow collection*

the island of Skye. Human and natural obstacles, however, were to ensure that the railway which eventually opened in 1870, was, in two distinct areas, much different from that originally envisaged.

At the eastern end, Sir William Mackenzie, leader of a group of local landowners, objected to the railway being routed over four miles of his land and within a few hundred yards of his Coul House, by Strathpeffer. As a result, the new line was forced into a northerly deviation, bequeathing railway operators a four-mile climb, much of it at a taxing 1 in 50 gradient via the Raven Rock (also known as the Ravens' Rock) and, in the process, omitting a station in Strathpeffer, the largest settlement between Dingwall and Kyle.

At the western end, the projected cost of blasting through ancient Torridonian sandstone, and also negotiating the indented coastline towards Loch Alsh, led to the new railway being terminated 10 miles to the east, at Strome Ferry on Loch Carron.

This proved a far from ideal harbour, being subject to strong currents and tides but, from the first day of passenger railway operation, connecting steamers plied their way from the new pier to Portree on Skye and Stornoway on Lewis. For passengers and goods from Glasgow, transport was transformed as the new route eliminated the lengthy sea passage round the Mull of Kintyre and past the Inner Hebrides.

Strathpeffer's touristic popularity continued to grow but, with its notional station being one-and-a-half miles distant up the steep road to Achterneed, the pressure increased for a railway serving the heart of the large spa village. A branch line was opened from Fodderty Junction, on the western outskirts of Dingwall, to Strathpeffer in 1885, five years after the Dingwall & Skye Railway

The photographer's son posts a letter in a former Highland Railway mail van about to depart north from Dingwall on 24 April 1952. Letters could still be posted in 'Travelling Post Office' coaches on the Highland Main Line until as late as the 1980s. *HC Casserley*

had merged with the Highland Railway which had been created in 1865. Ironically, the cantankerous Sir William Mackenzie would no longer be an objector, as he had died shortly before the opening of the Dingwall-Strome Ferry railway.

The combination of difficult currents for shipping at Strome Ferry and the threat posed to Skye and Lewis traffic by the authorisation of the West Highland Railway from Glasgow to Fort William in 1889 (with the prospect of the line in due course reaching the far west coast), led to the Highland Railway securing powers in 1893 for the extension westwards to Loch Alsh. Heavy engineering works between 1893 and 1897 eventually took the railway to Kyle, where the station site was blasted out of solid rock and a new pier provided for ships to Skye and the Outer Hebrides.

## The impact of the railway

The new terminus at Kyle was served by a 64-mile single-track railway from Dingwall (82 miles from Inverness), with crossing loops at seven of the eleven intermediate stations. Traversing largely unpopulated countryside – the main traffics would always be generated by the eastern and western termini – the line has ever since had a modest train service. Two or three trains daily in each direction (summer and winter) sufficed from the beginning through to the early 21st century. It was a tough railway to operate – with many changes of gradient and considerable curvature – but its wider economic and social impact was enormous.

The Achnasheen signalman surveys the mid-day scene when Up and Down trains crossed at this otherwise lonely railway outpost, in a photo thought to have been taken in the mid-1960s. The mailbus is ready to depart for Gairloch, Aultbea and Laide on the west coast. The sea cadets will doubtless be heading for the naval base at Aultbea. *David Lawrence/Photos from the Fifties (historical details courtesy of Iain MacDonald)*

The railway revolutionised the cattle trade in the Highlands. The beasts had previously been driven to the great southern markets, such as the Falkirk 'trysts', along a system of drove roads, over which a journey could take several weeks with the cattle arriving at market in a consequently poor condition. By contrast, rail could deliver livestock to market in a few days or less, and in good condition.

The arrival of the railway also transformed the fishing industry, opening up new markets for fresh fish in the south, notably herring from the seas west of Kyle, and salmon caught inland. The latter would be increasingly associated with the 'hunting, shooting and fishing' economy which developed over large tracts of land devoted to 'deer forest' rather than sheep: a response to falling wool prices and the development of refrigerated transport from Australia in the mid-1870s.

The new development contributed to the growth of tourist passenger traffic, but it was not only the 'shooting box' economy (a traditional description of the deer-hunting practice) which was opened up by the railway. *The Oxford Companion to British Railway History* (2003) records: 'The railways of Britain played a central role of converting tourism from an elite experience which had been enjoyed only by the monied few, into a mass phenomenon in which all classes and sections of society participated.' Among the previously isolated regions which were now opened up to less intrepid travellers were the Highlands. Of ten Highland Railway tours advertised for the 1896 season, no fewer than seven involved trips on the Dingwall & Skye line, often linked with steamers and/or horse-drawn coaches. And with the extension to Kyle, and its short ferry crossing to Skye, the line would come to be a fixture on British railway touring itineraries, which it remains to this day.

The former 'Devon Belle' observation car at the rear of the first train of the day from Inverness to Kyle on 21 July 1961, soon after diesel had displaced steam on the Kyle line. The train has just crossed the Blackwater Viaduct on the south side of Loch Garve, and is heading towards Garve. *Peter Tatlow*

As with many railways across Britain, the Kyle line soon also developed staple markets in the transport of coal and Royal Mail traffic. Goods and parcels were handled at the majority of stations along the line, notably at the exchange points for connecting buses to west coast locations isolated from the railway. These exchange points included Garve (for Ullapool), Achnasheen (for Gairloch) and Strathcarron (for Lochcarron, Shieldaig and Applecross). Schemes to extend the railway from Garve and Achnasheen westwards, through sparsely inhabited and unproductive country, came to nothing.

## War service

The strategic importance of the railways in wartime had been realised as early as 1855 in the Crimean War. In 1912, as the political situation across Europe worsened, the Government formed the Railway Executive Committee (comprising General Managers of the largest railway companies) which was ready to run the system if war was declared.

When World War One broke out in August 1914 this Committee took immediate charge, its attention soon turning to the far north of the United Kingdom where Britain's Grand Fleet, consisting of 96 ships and 70,000 men, was based at Scapa Flow in Orkney. Also, a large repair port was established at Invergordon on the Cromarty Firth. PJG Ransom records in *Iron Road* (2007): 'For the Highland Railway, the effect was as though a new city had materialised at its northernmost terminus.'

Unusually double-headed, a westbound train enters Achanalt loop on 21 July 1961, hauled by two 'Birmingham Railway Carriage & Wagon' Type 2 diesels. Five years later, as one of the economies following the reprieve of the line from the Beeching axe, the loop was removed, leaving a 16-mile, single-line section between Garve and Achnasheen. *Peter Tatlow*

To emphasise the Highland Railway's importance to the War effort, Inverness became a centre for the distribution of ammunition to the Grand Fleet, the weaponry being routed from 1915 over a new branch line to the town harbour. In August 1916, Inverness and the whole of the Highland region to the north and west, was declared a special military area.

Following the entry of the USA into the War in April 1917, the Allies decided to lay a minefield over the 230 miles from Orkney to Norway. The materials were manufactured in the USA and shipped to the west coast of Scotland at Corpach and Kyle for assembly at two US naval bases: in Inverness and at Dalmore, just south of Invergordon. Materials for the latter base were landed at Kyle and then transported by three or four special trains daily for around a week after the arrival of the fortnightly ships. The Admiralty commandeered the entire line from Kyle to Dingwall, with the Highland Railway allowed to run only one train daily in each direction for passengers and mails. All goods traffic for the islands was re-routed by ship from Glasgow.

## Grouping and nationalisation

By the end of the War, the unified railway had proved its capabilities, and it seemed unlikely that the system would revert to its former structure of more than 100 separate companies.

The 1921 Railways Act provided for the grouping of all Britain's railways into four companies, the largest of these being the London, Midland & Scottish Railway (LMS) which, within Scotland,

The diminutive Glencarron Platform – originally a private halt for the local laird's nearby Glencarron Lodge – was closed in 1964, but its short platform and tiny waiting shelter still survive in 2017. *David Fasken*

incorporated the Highland, Caledonian and Glasgow & South Western. The LMS would extend over 7,500 route miles, to which the Highland contributed 500 miles.

The economics of overland transport had also changed since pre-War days. In the 1920s mass production brought motor cars to the middle classes. Bus services expanded greatly (the first between Inverness and Dingwall being introduced in 1924), taking advantage of their greater flexibility over rail, and war-surplus lorries also contributed to a growing challenge to the railway's dominance in goods transport. Railway companies were further undermined by the impact of the 1926 General Strike, when the availability of alternative bus and lorry service gave additional impetus to these modes of transport.

Britain's railways came out of World War Two in a similarly exhausted state to that which they had experienced in 1919. However, the railways had again demonstrated the benefits of unified control and, following the landslide Labour victory in the 1945 General Election, it came as no surprise when the British rail system was fully nationalised in 1948.

Public ownership brought few early changes to the Kyle line, other than the closure of the Strathpeffer branch to passengers in 1946 and to freight in 1951. But by the mid-1950s rural railways throughout Britain were facing a growing threat from increasing household affluence and the resultant growth in car ownership, with the number of cars nationally more than doubling between 1933 and 1953.

In 1960, as an economy measure, British Railways (BR) closed 20 of the 41 passenger stations along the 168 miles of the Far North Line, including all seven intermediate stations between Inverness and Dingwall served by Kyle trains. The majority handled tiny numbers of passengers but, although

Hanging out of the window used to be a railway photographer's delight. This sketch is based on a photo taken from the rear of the mid-morning train from Inverness to Kyle, approaching the Raven Rock. *Merrill MacWilliam (from a photo by David Spaven)*

Beauly and Muir of Ord were surprising closures in population terms (and would eventually re-open), the combined frequency of Far North and Kyle line services – just seven trains a day in each direction – was poor competition for the half-hourly bus.

## The diesels arrive

One of the positive outcomes of nationalisation, and specifically BR's 1955 Modernisation Plan, was the replacement of steam by diesel.

The Highlands were located further from major coal fields than was almost any other part of Britain. The opportunity to eliminate expensive haulage of locomotive coal to the north, combined with the undoubted speed, operating cost and maintenance cost benefits of a switch to diesels, led to some of the earliest British diesels beginning trials on the Far North Line in 1958. By 1962 the entire rail network based on Inverness had been dieselised.

As early as 1914, a Scottish railway company – the Caledonian – had deployed a luxury observation car with large windows to allow tourists to make the most of the dramatic lineside scenery between Glasgow and Oban, but the spread of the motor car would soon undermine the economics of rail-based tourist excursions. After World War Two, the nationalised railway did fight back, with summer trains conveying a tail-end observation car between Fort William and Mallaig from the 1956 summer season onwards. Further panoramic observation cars were progressively introduced on lines

A multi-purpose railway: in the late 1960s Kyle station saw not only passengers, but also newspapers, parcels, Royal Mail and freight traffic. There were also connections to MacBraynes Buses (*top left*) and the Skye and Stornoway ferries. Today, there are only passengers and bus connections. *Frank Spaven*

in the West Highlands, culminating in 1961 in the arrival on the Kyle line of a car originally from the *Devon Belle*, a short-lived, post-War Pullman train of the Southern Railway.

## Dr Beeching arrives on the scene

Before the advent of significant road competition, a railway could make large profits on some part or parts of the service and then cross-subsidise. But by 1960 the large profits had disappeared, and the retention of loss-making services was driving the railway into further deficit.

So wrote retired senior railway manager RHN Hardy in *Beeching: Champion of the Railway?* BR's deficit in 1960 was £63.2m, the largest since losses were first recorded in 1956. In today's prices, this is around £1.3bn, or just one third of the cost to the taxpayer of supporting the privatised rail system. However, in 1960 the Government was alarmed, and in due course Dr Richard Beeching, Technical Director of the chemicals giant ICI, was appointed as Chairman of the British Railways Board.

Beeching came with an enviable reputation for thorough and clinical analyses of business problems, and he was soon applying himself single-mindedly to the railway problem in general, and specifically how to ensure that BR would break even financially over a five-year cycle, as now charged by the Government.

*The Reshaping of British Railways* – 'the Beeching Report' – was published on 27 March 1963. Closure of loss-making lines had been gathering pace nationwide for several years, and there was

A freight train from Kyle to Inverness heads towards Duirinish in the mid-1970s. The photo is thought to have been taken after the Stornoway ferry switched from Kyle to Ullapool in 1973, following which freight to Kyle was conveyed on the early morning 'mixed' train from Inverness, the wagons returning on a once-weekly freight train. *Frank Spaven*

widespread expectation that Beeching would propose many service withdrawals. But the scale of the proposals in his 148-page report came as a shock. Passenger services were to be withdrawn from 5,000 route miles, and over 2,000 stations would be closed across Britain.

The suspicions of the many pessimists in the north of Scotland were confirmed. Within the 35 pages of lists of routes and stations which were to lose their passenger services was the entire rail system north of Inverness. The 38 stations and 232 miles of the Far North and Kyle lines represented the largest rural route network to be threatened across Britain. But the Highlands was not slow to react.

On 29 March 1963, in an editorial on the Beeching Report, the *Inverness Courier* proclaimed: 'Today this country is facing the greatest crisis it has ever had to face in peace.' Just 15 days after Beeching unveiled his report, a conference held in Inverness by the Highland Transport Committee unanimously passed a resolution deploring and opposing the proposed withdrawal of passenger services. A broad-based campaign was quickly put in place – encompassing Local Authorities, trade unions, political parties, the media and the public at large – and was in due course encapsulated by the headline-grabbing 'MacPuff' campaign, led by farmers and industrialists.

Behind the scenes, many Scotland-based governmental bodies were arguing the economic and social case against closure, which was being pushed by the London-based British Railways Board and Ministry of Transport. A key player was my father, Frank Spaven, whose planning officer role at the Scottish Office involved analysis of the regional development implications of the Beeching Report. His 2003 obituary in the *Scotsman* credited him with being 'instrumental in saving the bulk of the Highland rail network'.

An official visit (via Duirinish station and the railway track) – presumably on a Sunday, when no trains operated – to the proposed oil platform construction yard site at nearby Drumbuie by the Public Inquiry team, witnesses, objectors and supporters. The scheme was rejected by the Scottish Office in 1974, and an alternative, less controversial, site was developed on the north side of Loch Carron at Kishorn. *Frank Spaven*

The multi-purpose railway to Kyle was central to the economic and social life of its route corridor from east coast to west coast, carrying not only passengers, but also daily freight, newspapers, parcels and Royal Mail. The parallel roads were inadequate (largely single-track) and people forced off the rails would be faced with lengthy, uncomfortable bus journeys. By April 1964, the arguments against closure had become politically irresistible, and the Government refused consent to withdrawal of passenger services.

Unsurprisingly, local media reaction to this announcement was joyous. The *Inverness Courier's* editorial summed it up: 'The Highlands have won a great victory'. The newspaper reported the reaction of one of the key campaigners from the West:

Mr Torquil Nicolson [from Plockton], Ross and Cromarty County Councillor, who opposed the closure of the Inverness-Kyle line – "There could be no better news for the west. This line should never have been on the closure list. It has caused us a lot of worry. It will be a new lease of life to Skye as well as the mainland. We could not have survived the blow had our railway link been severed."

### A new lease of life

The joy was justified, but the need for economies in rail operation was unavoidable. Minor stations were closed at Achterneed, Glencarron and Duncraig (the latter officially re-opened in 1976,

A tranquil Inverness coal yard, looking south toward the passenger station in the winter of 1974–5. After coal traffic ceased in the mid-1990s, this location handled the pioneering Safeway supermarket traffic by train from Central Scotland. *David Spaven*

although it had remained informally open ever since 1964). By 1966, all the intermediate stations between Dingwall and Kyle had been de-staffed, and every alternate crossing loop had been removed: at Achterneed, Achanalt, Achnashellach and Stromeferry (as it was now known in railway parlance).

A much less acceptable economy came after the 1967 summer season, with the cessation of regular operation of observation cars on all the scenic routes in the West Highlands. BR claimed that the existing coaches were life-expired, and that the revenue from them could not justify the cost of building new ones. Given that 50 years later all four were still either in revenue-earning service on heritage railways in England, or undergoing further restoration work, this was an outrageous claim, which represented the worst of post-Beeching management negativity towards surviving rural routes.

Despite the 1964 reprieve, the Kyle line was still not safe from threats. The new A890 road from Strathcarron to Stromeferry, running alongside the railway on the south side of Loch Carron, was opened in 1970, and plans were afoot to switch the Stornoway ferry from Kyle to the shorter route from Ullapool. And in 1971 the Government advised that the grant subsidy to maintain the rail service would be withdrawn at the end of 1973. But the road alternatives were still inadequate mainly due to winter weather problems and summer tourist congestion. A major campaign was once again mobilised.

This time round, BR management were pro-active in the face of closure – not wanting to take the blame for yet another cut in the network – and a promotional campaign was launched for the 1972 season. No fewer than 23 charter trains traversed the line in 1973: some from as far afield as London, Bristol and Crewe, reflecting a growing nationwide awareness of the scenic attractions of the line, as well as a wish to travel the route before its threatened closure. In mid-1973, with the fast-developing

A busy freight railway in 1977. Locomotive No. 26 032 shunts wagons of steel reinforcing rods at Kyle prior to hauling these to Stromeferry, for transfer to barge conveyance for the short sea haul to the Howard-Doris oil platform construction yard at Kishorn. *Bill Roberton*

North Sea oil industry investigating a site by the Kyle line (at Drumbuie, between Duirinish and Kyle) for oil platform construction, the rail closure was deferred for a further year.

Drumbuie did not proceed – due to opposition from the National Trust for Scotland and others – but a platform construction yard was established at nearby Loch Kishorn, served by barges conveying cement, steel and other materials from a new pier railhead at Stromeferry. And in mid-1974, passenger train services between Inverness and Kyle were once again reprieved by the Government.

With another new lease of life, the railway could confidently bid for new traffic. Regular freight continued until 1983, and between 1979 and 1994 various models of observation car adapted from traditional rolling stock were deployed on the route until the arrival of rail privatisation.

### Disaster avoided

The need for economies never disappeared and, in 1984, an innovative radio signalling system (controlled initially from Dingwall, later Inverness) replaced staffed signal boxes at Garve, Achnasheen, Strathcarron and Kyle. The next big economy – and associated service improvement – was scheduled for summer 1989, when new 'Sprinter' diesel units were due to replace traditional locomotive-hauled trains.

But perhaps the most dramatic – and certainly the most unwelcome – event in the history of the railway north of Inverness occurred on 7 February that year, when unprecedented flood waters destroyed the viaduct carrying the line over the River Ness. Fortunately, a quick decision was made

Not your typical West Highland scene. Cement silos and rail wagons at Stromeferry on 25 August 1977, during a relatively short-lived freight boom for the Kyle line, while heavy freight for the Kishorn oil platform construction yard was required to arrive direct by sea or rail plus sea. *Bill Roberton*

to reconstruct the bridge, and in the meantime the new diesel units were conveyed by road to a new operating base at Muir of Ord, allowing train services to continue on the temporarily marooned North Highland network.

The new Ness Viaduct opened on 9 May 1990, both for regular passenger services and for charter trains, increasingly enhanced by new local commuter trains also serving re-opened stations at Muir of Ord (1976), Beauly (2002) and Conon Bridge (2013).

Typically, more than 20 charter trains – including the luxury *Royal Scotsman* land cruise – annually traverse the Kyle line, but the route's capacity to handle these trains (bringing valuable visitor spend to the area) is limited by the short-sighted removal, in 1988, of the crossing loop at Lentran, mid-way between Inverness and Muir of Ord. Rail campaigners are currently pushing for reinstatement of this facility, allowing more trains to be introduced, and improving the reliability of the current timetable.

The year 2000 saw the replacement of the original Sprinter units by Class 158 'Express Diesel' units displaced from inter-city services. Although higher-powered than the replaced trains, they were far from the cutting edge of rail travel, with relatively cramped interiors, and prone to engine faults and air conditioning failure. The Inverness-based units – which continue to serve the Kyle and Far North Lines – were subsequently refurbished to accommodate more bikes and luggage and to provide a better match between seats and windows.

In 2001, all-year Sunday trains were introduced for the first time, and in 2008 – encouraged by HITRANS, the regional transport partnership – the Kyle line's timetable reached its best ever frequency, with four trains daily in each direction from Mondays to Saturdays.

Hotels and other visitor accommodation often promote their proximity to the Kyle line. One which couldn't be much handier is Strathcarron Hotel – with its railway-themed 'totem' signs – seen from the station in April 2017. *David Spaven*

In 2015, the ScotRail franchise was taken over by Abellio, a subsidiary of the state-owned Dutch railways. Its commitments to the Scottish Government include promotion of 'Great Scenic Rail Journeys' over six Scottish rail routes, including the Kyle Line. While there is no early prospect of the return of the 1950s-60s halcyon era of observation cars, the Class 158 units will be further refurbished and there will be dedicated tourism 'ambassadors', trained by VisitScotland, to provide information on the attractions, history and journey connections.

One hundred and twenty years after its opening through to Kyle, the Dingwall & Skye Railway has never been more dependent on its tourist business. The line remains one of the outstanding scenic rail journeys in Europe, passing through breathtakingly desolate countryside, before weaving its way beside Loch Carron and Loch Alsh for its dramatic arrival at Kyle's railway pier.

It is a safe, civilised and sustainable way to travel conveniently from east coast to west coast, avoiding the stresses and strains of car travel, although ScotRail's trains could never be described as breathtaking or world-beating. Is it too much to hope that the Kyle line and other deep-rural British railways will eventually be graced by purpose-built tourist trains – with observation cars – as routinely enjoyed today on scenic rail routes in Switzerland, the USA and Canada?

## Tales of 'a liquid railway'

In the Highlands, the homeland of whisky, alcohol long played a big part in the daily life of the railway – in every sense. These tales reflect the informal consumption, rather than the formal transportation, of the 'amber nectar' in past times.

In the early 1970s, I was part of a group from Edinburgh University who decided to take a trip on the train from Inverness to Kyle. At the first stop, Dingwall, a couple of us thought we'd try to hitch a cab ride, and ran up the platform to approach the Driver, who was in good form, and told us to jump into the back cab of the Class 26 diesel.

It was a cracking day and we hung out of the windows on the exhilarating 1 in 50 climb to the Raven Rock summit. Soon we began to notice small green cylinders flying out of the Secondman's window. This was the driver's mate swigging liberally from the distinctively coloured cans of McEwan's Pale Ale, a favourite tipple in that part of the world.

We continued the journey unperturbed – the Driver himself didn't seem to be drinking – but were interrupted suddenly at Achnasheen station, where the trains on this single-track line cross each other. The Secondman burst into the cab: "Lads, the Area Manager's getting on the train – you'll have to get down on the floor and hide!" Sure enough, the bowler-hatted BR official was striding up the platform and we had to get out of sight – quickly. At Kyle, we sneaked out of the cab without being spotted.

Achnasheen – which comprised little more than the station and adjacent hotel, surrounded by bogland – was a popular watering hole for rail passengers. The advertised timetable had plenty of slack to allow for late running, and particularly in the evening – when the last trains of the day crossed – there would often be an opportunity to jump off and grab a swift dram in the convivial hotel bar. Train crew were in the habit of putting their heads round the door to alert 'droothy' passengers when the trains were ready to head off east and west. On one occasion, David Fasken and I found that the custom could become even more sociable, when we shared a quick darts match and a pint with the Driver and Secondman of our Inverness-bound train! Sadly, the hotel burned down in 1995.

On another occasion on the Kyle line, my father and I returned from a walking trip at Achnasheen on 2 January, the first day of train service in the New Year. Our train – the last of the day to Inverness – drew to a halt at Garve (the lonely station and last passing loop before Dingwall), immediately adjacent to the signalman's office in the platform building. There – stretched out on his back on a wide table – was the big Garve signalman (well known as a caber-tosser at Highland Games throughout the region, but whose name I have diplomatically omitted). The train's Secondman calmly worked the signalling instruments for permission to proceed on the single-track section ahead, 'got the road' from the Dingwall signalman, and returned to the train, leaving one sozzled signalman to his dreams.

Eventually, of course, in response to health, safety and litigation concerns, the culture changed out of all recognition. This reached its apotheosis in 1993 when a Doncaster rail clerk – whose job never took him near the operational railway – was disciplined for drinking a half pint of lager at a farewell pub lunch on his last day of work. The pendulum had swung too far in the opposite direction, and the grassroots of the railway rose up in protest. The clerk was in due course cleared, but the railway's relationship with alcohol was now firmly, and for evermore, a strictly business one – bringing in high-capacity wagonloads of wine from France to national distribution centres in the West Midlands, and sending out container loads of export whisky from bottling plants in Central Scotland to England's Deep Sea ports.

*David Spaven*

## CHAPTER TWO

# Preparing for your journey

The passenger train services between Inverness and Kyle are part of the ScotRail franchise, created by the controversial privatisation of Britain's railway in the mid-1990s. The current ScotRail franchise – paid for by the Scottish Government to the tune of £7 billion over ten years – is operated by Abellio, ironically a subsidiary of the state-owned Dutch Railways.

The ScotRail web site – www.scotrail.co.uk – contains much of the information you will need about train times, station facilities and tickets. The printed 'North Highlands' pocket timetable is a useful companion to your journey, and is also reproduced on the ScotRail web site.

## When to travel

The weather in Scotland varies not only from season to season, but often also from day to day. Every season has its attractions, but the weather can be particularly benign in May or June, when typically there is less rain than later in the summer. September and October can also be good weather months.

The winter and early spring months have the advantage on sections where full-leafed trees obscure some of the immediate views from the train in summer and autumn. With Inverness and Dingwall being on the east coast, and Kyle on the west, it is not unusual for the weather to change *en route*, as the North Sea climatic influences give way to the Atlantic.

You may not have much flexibility in your choice of season for travel, but choosing a day other than a Friday and Saturday can help to avoid busier trains. For a trip from east coast to west coast, of the four trains daily there are essentially two day-trip train options: leaving Inverness at 08.55 or 10.56, returning from Kyle at 12.08, 13.46 or 17.13 (all times correct at the time of writing). On Sundays, at present, the 10.59 train from Inverness returns from Kyle at 15.12. The journey time is typically two hours 35 minutes from Inverness, and two hours from Dingwall.

### Buying your ticket/ticket types/seat reservations/assisted travel/bikes on trains

Tickets can be bought on the day of travel from ScotRail ticket offices at Inverness, Dingwall and Kyle or, in the case of the other (unstaffed) stations, from the guard on the train.

Advance purchase of tickets *can* save you money, and is available via the ScotRail web site or by phoning ScotRail Telesales (0344 811 0141 at the time of writing).

There is a relatively simple choice of ticket types for journeys wholly on the Kyle line (eg from Inverness or Dingwall), including:

- **Anytime Day Return:** a flexible ticket with no time restrictions on when you can travel, which can be booked in advance or purchased on the day of travel – but you must travel out and back

The stop sign at Strathcarron instructs eastbound train drivers on procedures under the line's Radio Electronic Token Block system, controlled from Inverness. The points at each loop are hydro-pneumatically operated so that they always lie towards the same loop line. *Merrill MacWilliam (from a photo by David Spaven)*

on the stated day. You may start, break and resume, or end your journey at any intermediate station along the route of travel. If you decide not to use your ticket to make all or part of your intended journey then you can apply for a refund, subject to a £10.00 administration fee. The Inverness-Kyle ticket offers a saving of around one third on the fully flexible Anytime Return (*see below*).

- **Anytime Return:** a fully flexible ticket, with the same conditions as the Anytime Day Return, except that the outward portions of Anytime Returns are valid for five days including the date on the ticket, and you can return anytime within a month.
- **Advance Purchase Single:** available on specified trains only, with no refunds.
- **Anytime Day Single:** a fully flexible ticket with no time restrictions on when you can travel, which can be booked in advance or purchased on the day of travel – but you must travel out on the stated day. Refunds available, subject to a £10.00 administration fee. This ticket type is only marginally cheaper than the Anytime Day Return.

All such tickets also benefit from the one-third Railcard reduction, eg for Senior Citizens or Young Persons.

Two 'Rover Tickets' are available, both encompassing the Kyle line as well as other rail routes, plus some bus and ferry services:

- **Highland Rover:** covering the Aberdeen-Inverness, North Highland & West Highland (from Glasgow) lines. Offers four days unlimited travel over eight consecutive days.

Scheduled ScotRail trains do not require any physical pulling of signal levers for normal operations through the line's various crossing loops. However, when additional trains – such as tourist charters – are operated to Kyle, then the train guard has to secure access by using this 'ground frame' beside the former signal box at Kyle. *David Spaven*

- **Spirit of Scotland Travelpass:** covering the entire ScotRail network. Offers four days of unlimited travel over eight consecutive days or eight out of 15 days.

Seat reservations can be obtained free of charge when you buy your travel ticket (reservations cannot be made for immediate travel). You can decide what type of seat you want by checking out Chapter Three below. If you require 'assisted travel' then ScotRail can arrange assistance if, at least four hours in advance, you call 0800 912 2901 (or text phone 18001 0800 912 2901 if you are hard of hearing).

Free bike reservations are available in advance, by booking online when you buy your train ticket/ calling telesales on 0344 811 0141/visiting one of ScotRail's staffed stations. The Kyle line's Class 158s have room for up to four bikes per two-car train set.

If you intend to walk any distance, good footwear and wet-weather gear are sensible precautions. Not all trains have buffet trolleys throughout the year so you may wish to take your own picnic. Up to two dogs, including guide dogs, on a lead are free of charge.

ScotRail's pocket timetable will allow you to keep track of timekeeping, and topographical maps such as the Ordnance Survey 'Landranger' series (Sheets 25, 26 and 33) will help you to appreciate the view from your window.

*Check that the travel/ticket conditions summarised above are applicable before you make a booking.*

# CHAPTER THREE

# Making the most of your journey

The journey to Kyle can be a thrilling experience, but it starts in a mundane manner: if you are joining the train at Inverness, you will need to insert your ticket in the electronic ticket barriers which separate the station concourse from the platforms. Your train for Kyle will depart from Platform 5, 6 or 7. Fortunately, all the other stations on the line are free from electronic control, so you can come and go as you wish.

## Your train: what you should know

The standard ScotRail train serving the Kyle line is the Class 158 diesel unit (with the engines slung under the floor) in combinations of 2-car (2-carriage/coach) or 4-car formation.

Each car has two sets of external doors, one at each end. These are twin 'plug doors', which move out and along the side of the train once centrally unlocked by the guard and then individually activated by a passenger push-button. On the outside of the train the activating button is to the right of the doors, and is rather further away from the door than seems sensible.

Take care when at some stations: there can be quite a wide gap between platform and train, particularly where the platform is on a curve.

For passengers with a disability: given advance notice, ScotRail will provide a ramp and assistance to enable smooth wheelchair access to the train. Arrive in plenty of time before the train departs. The allocated location for wheelchairs is in the large multi-purpose space towards the end of one of the two coaches.

Once inside the train, you will find yourself in a vestibule, with the passenger accommodation to the left or right, through a set of twin sliding doors, again passenger-activated by a button immediately to the right.

The passenger accommodation comprises an open 'saloon' with seats on either side of a central aisle. Seats are predominantly grouped in 'bays' of four seats around a table (two facing towards direction of travel, two facing away from direction of travel), with the bay generally well matched to the window, thereby maximising viewing opportunities.

Other seats are 'airline' style, with two on each side of the central aisle either facing towards or away from the direction of travel. The view from the train is generally not so good from airline seats, due to high seat backs.

For the particularly discriminating passenger, avoiding being directly above the underfloor engines (towards the centre of the coach) might be an option, but this will be at the price of a slightly rougher ride above the wheels (towards the ends of the coaches). In practice, however, the levels of noise and vibration anywhere in the Class 158s are not particularly noticeable, as these trains are sealed air-conditioned units.

Towards the end of one of the two coaches you will find a large multi-purpose space for wheelchair users, large luggage and bikes. For most day-trip purposes, there is adequate room for smaller luggage items in the overhead racks directly above your seat, and also in the floor space between adjacent sets of four-seat bays. Don't leave luggage or bikes in the aisle, or blocking doorways, as this will obstruct the buffet trolley, impede other passengers, and could be a safety hazard.

Once you are settled into your seat, your thoughts may turn to toilet needs. There are two toilets per two-car 158 set, located at the 'inner' end of each car. One is a fully accessible facility, with door opening, closing and locking by push-buttons, while the other smaller toilet has a manual sliding lock.

Before and during the journey, you will hear a range of public address announcements. Some are pre-recorded to advise general information about the train and the stops it will make, while others are made by the guard for purposes such as providing advance notice for alighting passengers to move to the single door which is opened at the short-platformed stations at Beauly, Conon Bridge and Attadale. But be warned: despite more than two decades of privatisation, which originally promised a transformation of the customer experience, the quality of public address announcements remains inconsistent in terms of content and manner.

Of course, in many ways the rail system is a parallel universe, with its own distinct sets of rules, regulations, operational procedures and obscure jargon. So you may well be confused by some of the announcements:

- *'we are waiting for the road'*: this derives from the original British description of 'railroad', as still used today in the USA and Canada. It is a reference to waiting for the Inverness-based signaller to authorise your train to move forward, usually after a train coming in the opposite direction has arrived in the crossing loop beside your train.
- *'we are waiting for the Up train'*: in British railway parlance, 'Up' describes trains heading towards London (or Edinburgh), while 'Down' describes trains from London or Edinburgh. On the Kyle line, Up trains are eastbound, and Down trains are westbound.
- *'crossing loop'*: the short stretches of double track at Muir of Ord, Dingwall, Garve, Achnasheen, Strathcarron and Kyle stations which enable westbound and eastbound trains to cross on this otherwise single-track railway.
- *'RETB'*: Radio Electronic Token Block, the innovative signalling system whereby the Inverness-based signaller communicates directly with the train driver, thus controlling the movement of trains over the single-track railway to Kyle.

Most on-train railway staff are happy to help passengers make the most of their journey. While you are unlikely to see or hear the train driver, the guard will pass through the passenger accommodation to check tickets and provide travel information and, on many trains, a buffet trolley provides passengers with snacks and drinks at their seats. Check the timetable for availability.

A distinctive feature of the train journey west of Dingwall is the 'clickety-click' sound of the train's wheels on the joints between the rails. Once a familiar sound on train journeys, this reassuring rhythm

The author makes his request for the 12.08 Kyle-Inverness train to halt at Attadale on 4 April 2017. Six of the line's stations are 'request stops'. Attadale's station is adjacent to the mature gardens and woods of Attadale House. *David Fasken*

Image text:

Passengers must
not cross the line

Warning
Do not trespass
on the Railway
Penalty £1000

158714

has largely disappeared from inter-city routes where short (60 feet length) rails have been replaced by long stretches of continuously welded track.

If you'd like to know the speed of your train during the journey to Kyle, simply count the number of clickety-clicks in five seconds, multiply by eight, and you have the approximate miles per hour. Between Inverness and Dingwall the speed limit is 75 mph, but west of Dingwall – due to curvature and track condition – trains are not permitted to exceed 45 mph, dropping to 30 mph and less on the sinuous route section by the shores of Loch Carron and Loch Alsh.

Although the 158s are sealed, air-conditioned units, you will be conscious of engine noise on the steep climbs where the train has to work hard to reach various summits. The steepest gradients are 1 in 50: for example on the four-mile climb from near sea level on the outskirts of Dingwall to the 458-feet summit at the Raven Rock. The route is characterised by heavy gradients and frequent changes of gradient. Combined with the line's considerable curvature – which minimised the cost of construction by avoiding heavy earthworks to get through natural barriers – this makes for a taxing task for train drivers, but the constantly changing view adds to the scenic interest of the journey.

However, it isn't only gradients which slow down the train. There are ten public level crossings between Inverness and Kyle, with train speed restrictions varying from 10 mph to 40 mph. While the vast majority of level crossing accidents in the Highlands are caused by motorists, the railway is an easy target for over-regulation, adding significantly to some journey times. Taking a wider perspective, this can be viewed as an expensive indulgence of the negligence of motorists, and would almost certainly not be countenanced by rail industry counterparts on the continent and in North America.

At the intermediate crossing loops at Muir of Ord, Dingwall, Garve, Achnasheen and Strathcarron – where you can see lineside 'distant signal warning' boards and 'Stop Boards' instructing the driver to stop and obtain permission to proceed – the train comes to a halt. This is not only for passengers but also for the driver to exchange a radio-transmitted 'electronic token' with the signaller in Inverness. The token controls the system whereby only one train can operate at any one time on a single-track section.

Should you find that the train sits for longer than expected at any of the loops, this will probably be due to a late-running train travelling in the opposite direction. There are long stretches of single track on the Kyle line – up to 20 miles – and delays can occasionally be severe, but this line performs more reliably than its sister route to the Far North. Other locations where you may be delayed are on the approaches to Clachnaharry, on the outskirts of Inverness (where the railway crosses the Caledonian Canal on a swing bridge), or at Clunes (between Clachnaharry and Beauly) where 'intermediate signals' allow trains travelling in the same direction to follow one another on the single-track section stretching from Inverness to Muir of Ord.

Do not worry about the safety of your journey. Rail is by far the safest overland form of transport. At the time of writing, no passenger has been killed in a train accident anywhere on Britain's main line railways since 2007. Single-track rail operation in the Highlands is a long-established and well-developed practice, whose safety has been continuously refined and enhanced, in part through learning the lessons of train accidents in the Victorian era. If safety is your main concern, then the train is far and away the best method of travel from Inverness to Kyle. However, in the unlikely event of an accident or emergency, the guard will give the appropriate directions and instructions. There are also safety notices posted throughout the train, which the public address announcements will routinely invite you to inspect. You could be the first ever passenger to take up this invitation!

The train also offers comfort, with well-designed, supportive seats and the option to get up and stretch your legs. However, it is not unknown for the 158's air conditioning system to fail in the summer. If that happens, the guard will open emergency windows, so the journey will be noisier but less overheated. As these trains were introduced more than 25 years ago, you may well wonder why this problem has still not been finally resolved.

## Alighting at stations

One of the quirkier aspects of your journey is that six of the line's stations are 'request stops', where joining passengers have to signal by hand to the driver and, prior to the previous scheduled stop, alighting passengers must ask the guard for the stop to be made. This is a sensible economy measure but, in a small way, it is also a special part of the journey experience. Putting your hand out to bring a train to a halt is not a power available to the average British (or foreign) rail traveller!

*The request stops are at Lochluichart, Achanalt, Achnashellach, Attadale, Duncraig and Duirinish.*

Unlike, for example, in Germany, the guard will generally not advise which side of the train the platform is located at the next station. Travelling westwards, the pattern is as follows:

- on the left hand side: Beauly, Dingwall, Garve, Achnasheen, Achnashellach, Strathcarron, Attadale, Duncraig, Duirinish and Kyle
- on the right hand side: Muir of Ord, Conon Bridge, Lochluichart, Achanalt, Stromeferry and Plockton.

## Facilities at stations

ScotRail's 'North Highlands' pocket timetable lists in detail the facilities at each station (plus some 'connecting' bus and ferry services). In summary these are:

- staffed stations with toilets at Inverness, Dingwall and Kyle
- ScotRail pre-booking 'Cab&Go' taxi service at Dingwall and Kyle
- car parking at Inverness, Beauly, Muir of Ord, Conon Bridge, Dingwall, Garve, Achanalt, Achnasheen, Strathcarron, Stromeferry and Plockton
- cycle racks at all stations except Lochluichart.

In addition, there are refreshment facilities at the following stations (and Strathcarron Hotel, with its restaurant and bar, is immediately adjacent to the station):

- Inverness
- Dingwall (The Mallard bistro bar, and Tina's Tearoom)
- Kyle (Waterside Seafood Restaurant, and Kyle Station Platform Shop and Snack Bar).

## Buildings of interest

The Kyle line may be renowned primarily for the scenic attractions of grand, natural, and man-modified landscapes, but there is also much architectural and historical interest among those structures which survive from the days of the Highland Railway. These include many bridges (*see below*), but most obvious to train passengers are lineside buildings.

The Scottish Government agency, Historic Environment Scotland, has 'listed' eight structures of '"special" architectural or historic interest' on the line: these are 'Category B', ie 'buildings of regional or more than local importance; or major examples of some particular period, style or building type, which may have been altered.' The locations are:

- the canal swing bridge and the signal box at Clachnaharry
- the viaduct over the River Conon at Conon Bridge
- the station at Dingwall and a nearby railway warehouse
- the stations at Duncraig and Plockton
- the station and pier at Kyle.

In addition, there are three surviving (but unlisted) original station buildings at Garve, Achnasheen and Strathcarron. On your journey you may also spot some other buildings dating back to past eras of the railway. Keep your eyes peeled.

# CHAPTER FOUR

# The view from your window

The 82-mile journey from Inverness to Kyle of Lochalsh takes the rail traveller from Scotland's North Sea coast to the Atlantic. The scenery is stunning and diverse, and comprises five distinct geographical sections:

- *Inverness-Beauly-Dingwall*: a fast journey though largely flat and fertile countryside
- *Dingwall-Garve-Lochluichart*: long steep climbs and two big summits in mountain country
- *Lochluichart-Achnasheen-Luib Summit*: a switchback railway of changing gradients and sinuous curves
- *Luib Summit-Achnashellach-Strathcarron*: a steep drop to the sea
- *Strathcarron-Stromeferry-Plockton-Kyle*: coastal twists and turns to the terminus.

Our 'view from your window' commentary helps to explain the key geographical, historical and railway features, with locations identified in the text as 'to the left' or 'to the right' for the westbound passenger, facing the direction of travel. While sitting on either side of the train will afford you countless good views, on balance the right hand side is the most outstanding, particularly on the coastal section from Strathcarron to Kyle.

## Inverness-Beauly-Dingwall

The first 18 miles of the journey are, strictly speaking, on the Far North Line, which was opened in stages from 1862 to Dingwall until Britain's most northerly railway reached Wick and Thurso in 1874. The Dingwall-Strome Ferry line opened in 1870 and the extension to Kyle in 1897.

Trains to Kyle typically leave from Platform 5 or 6 at Inverness station. On your right you can see the modern signalling centres, which control the North Highland lines and the immediate vicinity of Inverness on the lines to Aberdeen and Perth. Beyond them is the stone-built former Lochgorm Works of the Highland Railway, now a major maintenance facility for diesel units. On your left, the little-used Platform 7 has been shortened, and the scene is now filled with an ugly intrusion of security fencing, parked cars and waste bins – not the ideal send-off for one of Britain's most scenic rail journeys.

On their departure, Kyle trains join the western end of the 'Rose Street Curve': the tracks forming the third side of the railway 'triangle' at Inverness which enable through charter and freight trains to bypass the passenger station terminus. To avoid going through complex statutory procedures for withdrawing regular passenger services over this stretch of track, a daily ScotRail 'parliamentary' or 'ghost' train from Kyle (departing 17.13) traverses the section from Rose Street Junction to Welsh's

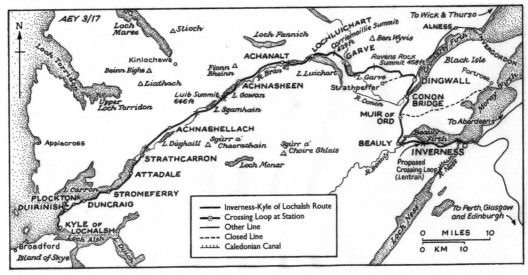

A remarkable survivor. It is striking how little the extent of the route network and stations has changed since 1912 (*see map on page v*), reflecting the dramatic victory of campaigners against the closure of the Far North and Kyle lines in 1964. Two minor branch lines have closed, four wayside stations have been lost between Inverness and Beauly, and west of Dingwall only two have gone. The loss of crossing loops has been more serious, notably in the case of the 13-mile section from Inverness to Muir of Ord, which has been single-track since 1988. *Alan Young*

Bridge Junction, reversing thence into the platforms for Aberdeen and Perth, then continuing to Elgin. From the earliest days of the Kyle Line until the end of regular locomotive-hauled trains in 1989, this was the operational practice for most trains from Kyle and the Far North.

Just beyond here, the remains of the former Inverness Harbour branch line can be seen trailing off to the right, now terminating in the former coal yard where the Safeway supermarket chain began their pioneering use of rail for trunk transport from central Scotland in 1999. The successor to this flow – Tesco supermarket supplies – today arrives by daily train at a larger purpose-built railhead to the east of Inverness station.

The train is now on an elevated stone structure and soon picks up speed across the River Ness on the modern viaduct opened in 1990 to replace the original bridge which was destroyed by flood waters in 1989. To the right is the often busy Inverness Harbour: until the 1970s the freight trains which trundled down the branch line beside the quays had to be preceded by a man carrying a red flag! You can still just see the 'tramwayed' track of the branch (closed in the early 1980s) set into the quay surface.

Once the train reaches the far bank of the Ness, below on the left you can catch a brief glimpse of the Merkinch ground of Inverness Clachnacuddin FC, the last Highland Football League team left in the town since the merger of Caledonian and Thistle and the renamed Inverness Caledonian Thistle's subsequent entry into the Scottish League in 1994. Further away to the south are Craig Dunain and Craig Phadraig, two distinctive hills looking down on the increasingly sprawling suburbia of Inverness.

With Ben Wyvis as backcloth, Type 2 (aka Class 26) No. D5344 eases its train across the B-listed Caledonian Canal swing bridge on a crisp autumn afternoon in 1966. *Merrill MacWilliam (from a photo by Frank Spaven)*

With the Black Isle (actually a peninsula) and the A9 Kessock Bridge to the right, the train is now slowing on its approach to the Caledonian Canal swing bridge, across which all passenger and freight trains are restricted to 10 mph. On a clear day, you will be able to see, beyond the fertile lands of the Black Isle, the great mass of Ben Wyvis, the highest peak in Easter Ross at 3,432 feet above sea level and the only 'Munro' (mountain of over 3,000 feet) on Scotland's east coast.

The 22 miles of the Caledonian Canal linking the east and west coasts – by way of Lochs Ness, Oich and Lochy – were engineered over 12 years by Thomas Telford, and were opened to traffic in 1822. In 1824, Joseph Mitchell of Forres, who had been a pupil of Telford's in London, was appointed as Chief Inspector of Roads in the Highlands. Mitchell and his partners Murdoch and William Paterson would later engineer virtually the entire Highland Railway system. Neil T Sinclair notes in *The Highland Main Line* (2013): 'Between 1803 and 1898 Telford, Mitchell and the Patersons were therefore responsible for almost all the new canal, road and railway infrastructure in the Central and Northern Highlands.'

The B-listed swing bridge is controlled from within the similarly B-listed Highland Railway signal box on the left, the only box left north of Inverness since the completion of radio signalling in 1988, and the most northerly operational box in Britain. Passing the beer garden of the Clachnaharry Inn, also on the left – and the site of a station which closed as early as 1913 (but whose footbridge still survives) – the train soon accelerates, running close to the alignment of the former A9 road on the southern shore of the Beauly Firth.

Framed by an original Highland Railway footbridge, this photo was taken on 31 March 1989 during the period when the railway north of Inverness was severed by the Ness Viaduct collapse. The photo looks south at Dingwall, with locomotive No. 37 417 *Highland Region* being serviced, and the B-listed former Highland Railway warehouse in the distance. *Bill Roberton*

Beyond the road overbridge at Clachnaharry, you may be able to spot the wider 'solum' (the area of ground within the railway boundary) where a second track was laid in 1913–14 as far as Clunes, a distance of six miles. The section between Inverness and Clachnaharry was never double-tracked, as this would have necessitated widening both the Ness Viaduct and the Caledonian Canal swing bridge. The double-track section was singled, post-Beeching, in 1966, leaving a crossing loop at Lentran, which in turn was taken out in 1988.

The Beauly Firth forms part of the Inner Moray Firth, a 'Special Protection Area' with extensive intertidal flats and smaller areas of saltmarsh. The rich invertebrate fauna of these flats, with beds of Eelgrass and Glasswort, provide important food sources for large numbers of wintering and migrating water birds (geese, ducks and waders). It is also the most northerly major wintering area for wildfowl and waders in Europe. In the far distance to the west, there is an inviting glimpse of the Fannichs mountain range.

The train slows again near the former station at Bunchrew (one of 20 stations on the Far North Line closed, pre-Beeching, in 1960), where we pass over the first un-gated and un-barriered level crossing to be opened on the British Rail network. Fifty years later, the crossing has barriers (and lights) but still the train has to reduce its speed to 35 mph.

The railway veers inland via the signalling system's 'token exchange point' at Clunes (where you may be able to spot the associated signage to the immediate left of the track), re-emerging by the Beauly Firth to cross the River Beauly on an imposing steel girder bridge, constructed in the early 20th century to replace the original timber structure.

Iron, steel and wood come together in style at Dingwall's B-listed station building, located on the Kyle and Caithness-bound platform. Dingwall is the only staffed intermediate station on the line. *David Spaven*

**Beauly** station was another of the 1960 casualties, but it re-opened in 2002 as Britain's smallest railway station. Just before we reach the modern station (which is on the left), look to the right for the original Highland Railway station building (now a private residence), where the local laird – Lord Lovat – had his own private waiting room. The small town of Beauly, whose name is derived from the French *beau lieu* (beautiful place), is the site of Beauly Priory, founded in 1230, which passed into the possession of Lord Lovat after the Reformation.

The railway is now heading north rather than west. After a short climb at 1 in 100 – the steepest gradient between Inverness and Dingwall – it reaches the site of another 1960 station closure, at Muir of Ord, which then re-opened in 1976. Muir of Ord was formerly the junction for the 13-mile Black Isle branch line to Fortrose: a relatively late arrival on the rail network which opened in 1894, closed to passengers in 1951, and saw its last freight trains in 1960. North of Muir of Ord, the distant mountain panorama to the west is jarringly breached by a collection of prominent wind turbines. Fortunately, to date, there are only two locations west of Dingwall where these giant industrial structures figure in the view from the train (east and west of Garve).

**Conon Bridge** station also closed in 1960, but re-opened in 2013 as part of a wave of expansion of commuter train services linking Easter Ross and Inverness-shire towns with Inverness. An Edwardian railway scheme which failed to come to fruition was the 18-mile Cromarty & Dingwall Railway (actually a misnomer, as the eventual junction with the Far North Line was planned to be at Conon), on which construction work began in early 1914, but was slowed by the start of World War One later that year.

THIS RAILWAY STATION WAS USED AS A
TEA STALL FOR SAILORS AND SOLDIERS FROM
20TH SEPTEMBER 1915, UNTIL 12TH APRIL 1919
IN CONNECTION WITH THE ROSS AND CROMARTY
COUNTY BRANCH RED CROSS SOCIETY.
DURING WHICH PERIOD 134,864 MEN WERE
SUPPLIED WITH TEA.

DINGWALL
STATION

The numerous sites of interest in and around Dingwall station include, on the main station building, this commemorative brass plaque celebrating a prosaic aspect of the line's massive role during World War One. *David Spaven*

Nevertheless, by late 1916 earthworks had been completed over 12 miles, and rails laid along the first four miles from Cromarty (with a locomotive and works train operating over the line). Early 1917 saw an abrupt end to construction when the 'permanent way' material was commandeered and removed by the Ministry of Munitions for use in France and Orkney. That was the end of the Cromarty & Dingwall Railway.

Shortly after Conon Bridge station, the railway crosses the River Conon on Joseph Mitchell's B-listed 1862 viaduct, then passes on the left the village of Maryburgh, with views towards the Cromarty Firth on the right, before the railway reaches the outskirts of **Dingwall**. Formerly the county town of Ross & Cromarty (the old county councils disappeared in 1975, and since 1995 a single local authority – Highland Council, based in Inverness – has controlled the entire mainland region from Lochaber in the south to Caithness in the north, including the Isle of Skye), Dingwall is now one of just four staffed stations on the entire 232-mile 'North Highland' rail network.

As the train slows towards the station, look out on the left for the three-storeyed, B-listed, former Highland Railway warehouse, originally used for the transfer of agricultural commodities from rail wagons to road vehicles, and now converted into flats. The railway at Dingwall saw an unprecedented volume of freight and passenger traffic during the 1914–19 war effort, HA Vallance in *The Highland Railway*, concluding that:

Had it not been for the Government control, and the existence of the powerful Railway Executive Committee, the Highland Railway would have been faced with an impossible task during the war

'Skye Bogie' No. 048 34 breasts the 458-feet summit at the Raven Rock, the narrow, rock-blasted defile demonstrating the work necessitated by the refusal of landowner Sir William Mackenzie to countenance the railway following the route via Strathpeffer. *Peter Tatlow collection*

Steam swansong. On 29 August 1960 an ex-LMS 'Black Five' battles up the last section of the four-mile, 1 in 50 climb to the Raven Rock summit with the first passenger train of the day to Kyle. *Peter Tatlow*

years. Fortunately, as part of a temporarily unified national railway system, it was able to rely for help on its larger partners. It was this fact alone that enabled the Company to avoid the complete breakdown that would have been little short of a disaster.

A profound verdict, perhaps, but the crucial national role of the railway north of Inverness between 1914 and 1919 also had its prosaic aspects, with a plaque on the wall of the main building at the B-listed station recording that 134,864 servicemen were provided with cups of tea there during the War. Below this plaque is a more recent addition commemorating the 2017 centenary of the 'Jellicoe Express' or 'Jellicoe Specials' – named after Admiral Sir John Jellicoe – which conveyed service personnel daily between London and Thurso, for Scapa Flow Naval Base, during both World Wars. Similar plaques have been erected at Inverness, Perth, Inverkeithing and Edinburgh Waverley stations.

## Dingwall-Garve-Lochluichart

The 17 miles from Dingwall to Lochluichart start close to sea level in fertile, well-populated country, but end up in barren mountainous terrain, relieved only by wide tracts of forest.

Immediately after Dingwall station, on the right, is the location of something of a 'rags to riches' story: Victoria Park, the home of Ross County Football Club, once of the Highland League, but now tussling with big-city opponents in the Scottish Premiership.

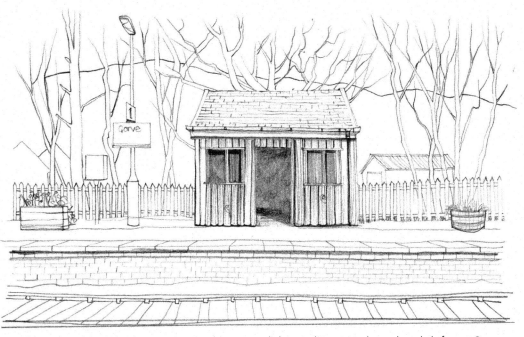

Several stations on the Kyle line boast attractive timber waiting shelters, in this case on the eastbound platform at Garve, seen in April 2017. *Merrill MacWilliam (from a photo by David Spaven)*

The Kyle line now veers west away from the Far North Line, crossing the former Dingwall Canal and soon traversing no fewer than three level crossings, where train speed is restricted to 20 mph for (road) safety reasons. Two miles from Dingwall, the railway reaches the former Fodderty Junction (for Strathpeffer, with the remains of the old branch line on the left), where we experience noticeable changes in the geography of the route, as the Kyle line begins its enforced detour away from Strathpeffer.

A sharp curve to the right takes the railway over the road to the north side of the valley of the River Peffery, and this is combined with an immediate change of gradient, from level to four miles of almost unbroken 1 in 50 gradient to Raven Rock summit. The 'clickety click' sound of wheels on rail joints is now an almost constant aural background.

As the train climbs steeply westwards, to the south we can see the distinctive shape of the Cat's Back ridge, the vitrified fort-topped Knock Farrell, and, below it, the lower-lying route which the railway to Kyle could and should have taken. But the climb to the line's second-highest summit (451 feet) is an exhilarating railway experience, and still presents a challenge for today's steam-hauled charter trains. Interestingly, for most of the line's history, westbound trains required 'banking' engines at their rears for this part of the journey, with the banker dropping off the train once the summit was reached. This practice continued until the end of steam in 1960–61.

A brief relaxation of the gradient takes us through the level crossing and former station at Achterneed (closed in 1964, and originally the station for the nearby spa village before Strathpeffer

Almost 150 years after its construction, the wide gap between tracks at Garve is still evident in this April 2017 view. In the distance, the A835 road to Ullapool crosses the railway at a level crossing. *David Spaven*

secured its own branch line in 1885), quickly resuming the 1 in 50 gradient on the final approaches to the line's first summit.

A precipitous 250-feet high cliff – where it is said that ravens hold their annual ball – forms a dramatic flank to the Raven Rock (874 feet) towering to the left and south above the railway. The line here runs through the narrow defile of Glenskiach, with Druim a'Chuilein (1,172 feet) to the north. Some 20,000 cubic yards of hard rock had to be removed in order to squeeze the railway through. A surviving description of a 19th-century 'footplate' (locomotive cab) journey memorably records that: 'The re-echoing of the heavy blasts from the chimneys while in the cutting are like continuous thunder peals.'

The Raven Rock was the scene of a potentially fatal accident, which brought renewed Government focus on regulating the Highland Railway's traditional practice of operating 'mixed' passenger and freight trains. In the 1880s, around half of all the timetabled Highland trains were mixed: a sensible consolidation of traffic on lightly-populated routes where the total traffic on offer was not substantial.

There were operational dangers, however, where, as was Highland custom, in order to simplify shunting of goods wagons at intermediate stations, the wagons were marshalled immediately behind the locomotive. As a result, there was no continuous braking system linking the locomotive and the passenger coaches which enabled all their wheels to be braked simultaneously.

In 1891, the Board of Trade issued an order to the Highland Railway, requiring all passenger vehicles on mixed trains to be marshalled next to the locomotive, so that the continuous brake might work on them. The order did not come into force until 1896, but was – for operational convenience – ignored

Skirting the shore of Loch Luichart, locomotives No. D5338 and D5125 haul the 'Scottish Region Grand Tour No. 17' towards Kyle on 15 September 1973. Tourist charter trains remain a staple traffic on the Kyle line today, but there are concerns that proposed road works alongside Loch Carron would result in the railway being restricted to light-weight ScotRail trains only. *Bill Roberton*

on 25 September 1897 when a coupling broke between two goods wagons on a Dingwall-Strome Ferry service (with four passenger coaches attached in the rear).

The 10 rear vehicles ran back down the steep gradient, overcoming the brake in the guard's van, and were only brought to a halt, after covering nearly six miles, when they crashed into level crossing gates just 200 yards from the junction with the Far North Line in Dingwall. This must have been a terrifying experience for all on board but, miraculously, the train was not derailed and the passengers were unhurt. By the turn of the century the Highland Railway was belatedly complying with the Board of Trade regulations…

If an ambitious 1970s plan had come to fruition, the Raven Rock would have been the junction with a continental-style electrified 'rack railway' taking passengers to a new ski development on the slopes of the 3,432 feet-high Ben Wyvis. The proposal for the Dingwall & Ben Wyvis Railway, and an associated spur line from Achterneed to Strathpeffer and the new ski runs and winter sports facilities it would have serviced, was controversial, given the sensitive ecosystem of the mountain, which is now both a National Nature Reserve and a Special Landscape Area. Despite being granted outline planning permission in 1981 by Highland Regional Council, the Dingwall & Ben Wyvis Railway project never came to fruition, and nor did repeated initiatives in the late 1980s, mid-1990s and early 2000s.

Passing the remains (on your left) of a rail-served quarry abandoned at the start of World War Two, the railway drops down through the forested moorland of Rogie – with much evidence of recent timber harvesting – to the southern shores of Loch Garve and the four-span girder viaduct over the

The distinctive metal bridge on the reverse curve which takes the railway from the south side of Loch a' Chuillinn to the north side of Loch Achanalt, seen here on 5 April 2017 with the 13.46 train from Kyle heading away towards Inverness. *David Spaven*

Blackwater River. Across the loch can be seen Carn Fearina (1,408 feet) and beyond that Carn [sic!] Gorm (1,705 feet), and to the left of it, Meill Ruigh an Fhirich, topped by a radio mast. In Gaelic, Garve means 'rough loch', and Loch Garve is over 100 feet at its deepest point.

Unfortunately, the view from the train along the side of Loch Garve is frequently obscured in summer by the recent, unmanaged growth of alder, ash and birch trees on the lineside. Surely this is an opportunity to replicate the good work done by a partnership on the Glasgow-Fort William line – involving Network Rail, ScotRail and the Friends of the West Highland Lines – to remove obstructive vegetation above Loch Long and Loch Lomond?

Since 1964, the first stop made by Kyle trains west of Dingwall has been at the small village of **Garve**, where passengers and mail were formerly detrained for the connecting bus to Ullapool. The original stone-built Highland Railway station building survives here (on the right, unfortunately now painted in shocking yellow), as do buildings of the same design at Achnasheen and Strathcarron. But most other old structures at Garve are long gone, including one of the two former signal boxes, now enjoying a new lease of life on the 'heritage' Strathspey Railway at Aviemore. Fortunately, the traditional lattice footbridge (manufactured at the Rose Street Foundry in Inverness in 1906) still provides a graceful means of access to the platforms, and both platforms have attractive (modern) timber shelters.

A unique feature of the rail layout here is the great width between the adjoining tracks of the crossing loop. This is the surviving evidence of an abortive scheme, planned during the early phase of

Locomotive No. 37 415 heads east from Achnasheen with an Inverness-bound train on 4 April 1988. A year later 'locomotive plus coaches' were replaced by lighter and more cost-effective diesel units. *Bill Roberton*

construction of the railway, to convey fishing boats up to 16 feet wide by train from the east to west coasts. Today, ScotRail trains cross at Garve just once a day, in the early evening.

Immediately north of the station was the only road overbridge on the original line to Strome Ferry, which was replaced two decades ago by a level crossing. Here, the express bus from Inverness to Ullapool, connecting with the Stornoway ferry, can still be caught several times daily, but today there is no formal 'connection' with the train. The line is level through Garve station but, as soon as the two tracks of the crossing loop converge to the west, the railway begins another fierce climb at 1 in 50 towards the 429 feet Corriemuillie Summit.

At a road junction a couple of miles north of Garve, the A835 veers north-east (then north-west) towards Loch Broom and Ullapool, while the A832 road (single-track at the time of the Beeching closure threat, but now of conventional width) closely follows the route of the railway towards Achnasheen.

Still in forested terrain, a steep descent from the summit takes the railway down to the northern shores of Loch Luichart, whose waters were raised some 25 feet by a 1954 hydro-electric power scheme. This had important consequences for the railway, requiring a two-mile realignment to the north, a new bridge of 100 feet span over the River Conon, and the construction of a new Lochluichart station. Just before the station, you can see (on the left) the alignment of the old railway, part-submerged under the loch. To the south-west – across the loch – you can see Sgurr a' Mhuillin (2,845 feet) and, to its right, Sgurr a' Ghlas Leathard (2,778 feet).

Locomotive No. 37 415 heads further east from Achnasheen with an Inverness-bound train on 4 April 1988. *Bill Roberton*

The 'new' station building (no longer in railway use) demonstrates that utilitarian, indeed ugly, architecture was firmly established well before the unlamented 1960s. Keep your fingers crossed that nobody will request a stop at Lochluichart, as the station is also flanked to the north by a bizarre, semi-abandoned junk yard of portakabins, lamp posts, satellite dishes, breeze blocks and flower pots. Yet the station sports a Keep Scotland Beautiful 'Bronze Award' plaque! Sometimes, the reality of the Highlands is very different from the hype of the tourist brochures.

For some reason, Lochluichart is the only station on the Kyle line without a cycle rack, but that doesn't explain why just 608 passengers joined and alighted trains here in the last recorded year (2015–16). Nor is Lochluichart the quietest station on the line.

## Lochluichart-Achnasheen-Luib Summit

Constantly changing gradients and sharp or sinuous curves characterise the next 15 or so miles of railway.

The line climbs into Strath Bran (Gaelic for 'valley of the drizzle'), along which the River Bran drains into the hydro-heightened waters of Loch Luichart, with Carn na Beiste (1,681 feet) to the right. Wide swathes of the strath are now forested, a noticeable contrast to the bare and bleak landscape of much of the railway's history. It is also a reminder that a native forest of pine and birch clothed this landscape for thousands of years until the arrival of timber extraction. Then, in the late

The original stone station building of the Highland Railway at Strathcarron – now unstaffed – is complemented by later additions, including the corrugated, iron-roofed former Post Office in the foreground, seen in April 2017. *David Fasken*

18th and 19th centuries, large-scale sheep faming and 'deer forest' initiated further dramatic changes in the Highland environment.

We soon reach the eastern end of Loch a Chuillin, where Achanalt hydro station is powered by the loch's waters and an adjoining 'salmon ladder' allows returning fish to reach their spawning grounds. One of the most photographed locations on this section of the line – particularly in those happy days when passengers could hang out of the train windows – is the reverse curve which takes the railway from the south side of Loch a Chuillin to the north side of Loch Achanalt.

The next station, Achanalt, has the dubious distinction of handling the fewest number of passengers on the Kyle line: only a total of 312 joined and alighted from the train in 2015–16. Of Britain's 2,253 stations, only 22 saw fewer passengers than Achanalt in 2015/16. Like Lochluichart, Achanalt is a request stop and serves little more than a handful of houses, but it was once an important staging point on the up and down alignment through Achnasheen to the summit at Luib.

Hill walkers have little to disturb them as they stride north from this utilitarian station through Lochrosque Forest to reach Loch Fannich, then follow its shores westwards before heading back south towards the A832 and Achnasheen. On the railway, immediately after the station (to the right) is a 'dry-staned dyked' cemetery, meaning that the 'dyke' (wall) does not use mortar to bind its stones together. Thereafter, the forest peters out, exposing a flat and bare strath across which the River Bran meanders, in sharp contrast to the neighbouring mountains.

At the western end of Strathbran is the isolated station and crossing loop at **Achnasheen**, roughly the halfway point between Dingwall and Kyle. Unlike at Garve, the width between the tracks is

Westbound passengers at Strathcarron can escape the elements in this corrugated iron-roofed waiting shelter on the Down platform, seen in April 2017. *Merrill MacWilliam (from a photo by David Fasken)*

standard, known on the railway as 'the six foot', as opposed to the 'four foot' between the rails of each track. The plan to accommodate fishing boats on trains must, therefore, have been abandoned in the period between the construction of the two stations.

Here there is still an engineers' siding for track maintenance machines, and traditional wooden railway sleepers (the balks which underpin the rails). For many years, the main trains of the day crossed at the loop here, and regular passengers could duck into the adjacent Achnasheen Hotel (with a direct entrance from the station platform to the bar) for a swift dram, confident in the knowledge that the driver or guard, who were often fellow bar customers, would give them the nod when the trains were ready to leave.

During the line's halcyon years, two named trains connecting with steamers at Kyle – *The Hebridean* (westbound) and *The Lewisman* (eastbound) – exchanged their Inverness-based restaurant car (silver service and all the trimmings) at Achnasheen. While this was going on, another, more longstanding tradition was being enacted on and beside the eastbound platform, which was the interchange between the train and mail bus, with Achnasheen acting as the staging point for Gairloch and Poolewe on the west coast, and the passengers, parcels and newspapers also being transferred from rail to road. Today, there is one – non-connecting – bus a week at Achnasheen (from Dingwall) to the west coast.

Sadly, the hotel burned down in 1995, and these days, other than the nearby Ledgowan Hotel and the junction where the roads to Gairloch (A832) and Kyle (A890) part company, the station effectively *is* Achnasheen. Fortunately, the stone-built original Highland Railway station building has survived, as has the lattice footbridge connecting the two platforms.

A fine original iron footbridge links the two platforms at Strathcarron, seen here as the 08.55 Inverness-Kyle train draws to a halt on 4 April 2017. The train driver will then contact the signaller at Inverness to obtain the electronic token allowing the train to enter the 18-mile single-track 'block section' to Kyle. *David Spaven*

In 1973 when I began my life on the railway (in Invergordon, on the Far North Line), one of the first railwaymen I met was signalman Iain MacDonald, otherwise known as 'the Blackbird', reflecting his jet-black hair colour. Train drivers also often went by nicknames in those days. In Inverness there were, for example, 'the Bandit', 'the Cowboy' and 'the Crow', at least two of whom had earned their monikers through their driving style.

MacDonald was born and brought up in Easter Ross, where in 1952 he began work on the railway. Later, after National Service, MacDonald found that his old job had been filled, so he had to report to BR management at Inverness to find another post (which he was guaranteed). He was offered jobs at Struan, Strome Ferry or Achnasheen, 'none of which I fancied', so he decided to look for a job outside the railway in Easter Ross. But there were none:

> So I went back humbled and said I'd had a think about it, and yes, I was willing to come back to the railway service. And the response was: "Oh, we don't have Struan now, and we don't have Strome Ferry. The only place we can offer you is Achnasheen [*which of course was infinitely more isolated than Easter Ross*]." That did learn me.

After only three weeks' training at Achnasheen, MacDonald became a passed-out signalman, but he spent only 11 months at this lonely outpost. Nicknames were everywhere on the railway, and in 2016 he recollected that 'we had a Budgie when I was at Achnasheen. Some couldn't tell us apart, so we had a Blackbird and a Budgie working at the same station'. MacDonald's quick promotion to a Class 2

A classic photographic location on the Kyle line is just west of Attadale, where the railway sweeps through a long curve by the shores of Loch Carron, seen here on 5 April 2017 with the 12.08 Kyle-Inverness slowing in case of an Attadale request stop. *David Spaven*

relief signalman post at the metropolis of Inverness was a mixed blessing. One of the first signal boxes he learnt was Rose Street, controlling the tracks to Platforms 5, 6 and 7, the 'Rose Street curve' lines avoiding the terminus station, and a level crossing:

> You needed to watch your back when working in Inverness; there was always somebody willing to report you. On one occasion at Rose Street, I was sitting reading a book, and for some reason I had to stand up, still holding the book. Somebody spotted the book and reported that I'd been reading rather than working. I think I told management that it had been the Rule Book!

Today's modernised railway has no need for any signallers west of Inverness (other than at Clachnaharry to control the swing bridge). ScotRail trains are scheduled to cross at Achnasheen only once daily (in the mid-afternoon), but in the summer season any of the line's loops can be the location of a crossing with one of the charter trains for which Kyle is such a popular destination – including the luxury *Royal Scotsman* 'land cruise' service from Edinburgh, with its distinctive plum livery. You may need to save your pennies if you're tempted to sample this sumptuous elegance on wheels: prices start at over £4,000 for a five-day cruise. Other locomotive-hauled charter trains, with traditional dining, such as the occasional SRPS Railtours day trips from the Edinburgh area, are easier on the bank balance, priced at under £75 at the time of writing.

Immediately west of Achnasheen, the railway shifts to a southerly direction and crosses the River Bran on a recently repainted wrought-iron lattice girder bridge, with terraces of glacial deposits to be

Rock falls continue to obstruct the road and the railway on the shores of Loch Carron. The road and rail avalanche shelter constructed in 1969–70 is about to be entered by the 11.00 Inverness-Kyle train on 5 April 2017. *Merrill MacWilliam (from a photo by David Spaven)*

seen on the left. Here you can often spot deer – sometimes an entire herd – and further on (to the right) is a shooting lodge, occasionally visited by its own pet stag. On hot summer days, deer will cool off in the river flowing into the west end of Loch Gowan.

Gradients as steep as 1 in 55 take the line from Achnasheen to its highest point at Luib Summit (646 feet) which is also the watershed between rivers draining to the North Sea and Atlantic coasts. John Thomas, in *The Skye Railway*, describes the train journey around here:

> …passing on the way a succession of lochs [on the right] set like jewels in their own mountain basins. First came Loch Gowan and then [after the summit] Loch Sgamhain – Loch of the Lungs. In Loch Sgamhain lurked a water kelpie. It was well known in these parts that it devoured whole anybody unlucky to fall in – except the victim's lungs which floated to the surface.

Ahead (to the right) the strath is overlooked by the mountain masses of Carn Beag (1,804 feet) and, beyond that, Beinn na Fuisage (2,051 feet).

### Luib Summit-Achnashellach-Strathcarron

On the first stage of its 14-mile descent to the coast, the line drops steeply down Glen Carron – in places at 1 in 50 – but never very far from the River Carron. To the right, you may catch a glimpse of one of the many lineside huts (typically wooden, with rusty corrugated iron roofs) built to shelter

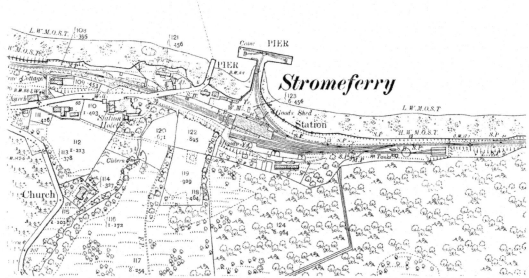

Extract from an Ordnance Survey 1:2,500 map made following the extension of the line to Kyle, but still showing the pier and engine shed with associated sidings at Stromeferry. From 1974 to 1977 a rail-connected pier served barges conveying cement and steel to the Loch Kishorn oil platform construction yard. *Peter Tatlow collection*

permanent-way men who traditionally walked the line several times a week. Today, track maintenance is largely mechanised, utilising engineers' sidings at Garve, Achnasheen, Strathcarron and Kyle, but once a week the track is still walked or reviewed from a road-rail Land Rover.

The surrounding country closes in on the railway around Glencarron Gorge, overlooked from the south by the 3,026 feet peak of Moruisg (on your left). You will briefly hear a quickening of the clickety-click rhythm as the train traverses a short section of 45-feet length rails, as opposed to the standard 60 feet. Where the line crosses from the south to the north bank of the River Carron, you can glimpse Glencarron Lodge on the right and, just after the bridge over the river, its former station on the left. In the early 19th century the inhabitants of the glen were cleared to make way for sheep, then the land was turned over to deer forest. In 1870 it was split between two estates, both of which proved troublesome for the railway.

Mr JR Shaw of Glencarron Lodge insisted on having his own private station, which was duly provided, and 'Glencarron Platform', with its passenger-operated semaphore signals, effectively served as a public station until its Beeching-inspired closure in 1964. Ironically, the 1974 Ministerial reprieve of the Kyle line and its stations specifically included Glencarron so, although no train ever calls there, in theory it is still open. The remarkably intact low platform and tiny wooden waiting shelter can just be spotted from the train. The recent restoration of the building in traditional railway colours was sponsored by the Small Stations Society, a body with a long track record of helping to preserve railway architecture across the Highlands.

There is a frontier feel in this 25 August 1977 photo of Stromeferry station, with the remnants of the original 1870 terminus building still clinging on, while the background is solidly industrial. *Bill Roberton*

Heading into Achnashellach Forest and towards the next station at **Achnashellach** ('the field of willows' in Gaelic), the line should have continued to hug the river on a largely continuous descent towards the sea, but Captain Tennant, the local landowner, did not view with enthusiasm the prospect of seeing trains from the front windows of Achnashellach Lodge. The railway was forced to veer northwards, crossing the public road and climbing at gradients of up to 1 in 60 to reach the initially private Achnashellach station. The obstructive landowner soon found the railway to be very much to his personal taste, however, as John Thomas records in *the Skye Railway*:

Within a month of the opening of the line Tennant, taking advantage of the new means of communication, staged an elaborate house party at Achnashellach. Two special trains were required to convey the guests from Dingwall to Tennant's private station. The normal charter fee for a special was 8s per mile. This Tennant refused to pay, but he stated his willingness to pay any reasonable charge decided on by the directors. The board reduced the charge to 4s per mile 'holding this as a special case but intimating to him that for any special trains run in future no deduction from the usual charge will be allowed.'

It was a grand party. It was said that 200 guests travelled on the special trains. But when it was over Tennant refused to pay the specially reduced charge claiming that it was still too high. The board reduced the fare to 1s 10d per mile which was the fee paid by the Skye company to the Highland for the hire of the trains. On that basis each traveller was getting almost 10 miles of travel for a penny. Tenant refused to pay even that modest amount. Two years later, at a board meeting

Steel-mesh netting clothes both sides of the massive cutting just east of Duncraig station, demonstrating the scale of engineering work required between 1893 and 1897 to blast the railway through the 10½ miles of tough terrain from Stromeferry to Kyle. Seen in April 2017. *David Spaven*

on 5 August 1873 Andrew Dougall [Secretary of the Dingwall & Skye Railway] reported that 'Mr Tennant has not yet paid for the two special trains run for him in 1871'. It was resolved to adhere to the modified charge intimated to him shortly after the trains were run. But by then Tennant had left the district. There is no evidence in the company's records that the charter fee was ever paid.

This was just one example of landowner attitudes in the Highlands and of the Dingwall & Skye Railway's evidently extreme deference to these people. But the changing gradients caused by Tennant's insistence on route diversion at Achnashellach contributed to a serious incident, HA Vallance recording in *The Highland Railway*:

An unusual accident occurred on 14 October 1892, at Achnashellach, on the Dingwall & Skye Railway. When the afternoon mixed train from Dingwall arrived, the engine was detached to do some [goods traffic] shunting, the weight of the coaches overcame the resistance of the brake in the rear van, which was out of order, and the whole train ran back down a steep gradient. It came to rest some distance up the succeeding rise, whence it moved forward once more towards the station.

Although darkness had fallen, the engine was sent back to pick up the train. It had proceeded some distance when it met the runaways moving in the opposite direction, and a violent collision ensued in which eight passengers were seriously injured.

This accident, like the mishap at the Raven Rock in 1897, eventually led to enforced changes in Highland Railway operating practice for mixed trains. The practice of conveying both passenger

The charming station at Duncraig (closed in 1964 but re-opened by British Rail in 1976), where the original octagonal wooden waiting shelter still survives, as seen in April 2017. *David Spaven*

coaches and goods wagons on one train remained a distinctive feature of Kyle line operations until the end of regular freight traffic in 1983. Latterly, the early morning Monday to Friday freight train from Inverness would convey a passenger coach immediately behind the locomotive – as first stipulated by the Board of Trade back in 1891 – with the freight wagons all returning from Kyle to Inverness on a once-weekly (Saturday) freight train. Since 1983 there have been only occasional freight flows, notably timber from Kyle to processing plants in the south.

Just west of the station platform a public right of way crosses the railway, leading by way of the dramatic Coulin Pass (to your right) through the mountains to Glen Torridon and the mighty peaks of Liathach and the Beinn Eighe National Nature Reserve. Close by the start of this old pony track is the former Achnashellach stationmaster's house (to the right of the railway). During the 1980s, a keen gardener took ownership of the house and over many years created a luxuriant garden, which was regularly open to the public. But visitors remember midges being an occupational hazard at this wet and wooded location!

West of Achnashellach, the glen widens out into a strath, with distinctive remnants of the ancient Caledonian Pine Forest stretching down to the shores of Loch Dughaill (on the left), overlooked by the imposing ridge of Creag an Eilein. A wrought-iron lattice girder bridge then takes the railway across the now-meandering River Carron before the train reaches the line's last intermediate crossing loop, at the tiny settlement of **Strathcarron**.

The station building here is of a similar design to those at Garve and Achnasheen, and the original footbridge survives. The formerly low platforms have been rebuilt, necessitating construction of a

An attractive stone over-bridge frames the deep cutting east of Duncraig station. *Merrill MacWilliam (from a photo by David Spaven)*

retaining wall between the new platform level and the lower entrance to the station building, which is now in private ownership. Like all the stations on the line – except for Achnashellach, Stromeferry and Duirinish – Strathcarron, with the encouragement of ScotRail, has been 'adopted' by local friends of the railway. The Strathcarron Hotel, with a bar and restaurant, is conveniently right beside the station.

When the railway opened, a road was built to connect the station with the east-west road a mile to the north, leading towards the most populous settlement in the district: **Lochcarron,** on the north shores of the loch of the same name. From the early days of the railway, a horse-drawn coach provided connections from the main train of the day to Lochcarron, and to Sheildaig and Torridon further north.

After World War One, D McLennan of Sheildaig began to operate a motor service conveying passengers and mail, and today its bus descendant continues to connect out of the first two train arrivals from Inverness at Strathcarron. The station's valuable railhead function is reflected in its annual patronage: of the line's 11 intermediate stations west of Dingwall, only Plockton saw more passengers in 2015–16.

### Strathcarron-Stromeferry-Plockton-Kyle

Until 1970, Strathcarron station stood at the end of the short stub of B856 road, bypassed by Kyle and Skye-bound main road travellers heading for the ferry across Loch Carron at Stromeferry, some miles

Plockton is one of three stations on the Kyle line where the original wooden station building survives. Seen in April 2017, the station is unstaffed, but the building now provides self-catering accommodation facilities for visitors. *David Fasken*

beyond the village of Lochcarron. To speed up the journey, a decision was made to build a new main road (what would become the A890) leading from Strathcarron station along the southern shore of Loch Carron to Stromeferry – eliminating the 10-minute ferry crossing, which had operated since the early 19th century, and avoiding a 140-mile road detour via Inverness.

This was to have consequences for the railway which are still being felt today – of which, more later – but here we can just note the road's level crossing which cuts across the two rail tracks west of Strathcarron's platforms. Not exactly Piccadilly Circus, but a lot busier than it was 47 years ago.

John Thomas in *The Skye Railway* sums up the imagined experience of a westbound train journey beyond Strathcarron on the line's opening day:

> The salt water of Loch Carron, the goal of the Dingwall & Skye promoters for six years, lay ahead. The train wound slowly round the contours of the loch shore, so close to the loch itself that a passenger could have dropped a stone into the water, while on the left of the track a curtain of rock rose high above the carriages. The passengers were unlikely to complain that the train took 30min to cover the last seven magical miles. At the end of the line came Strome Ferry pier with *Oscar* waiting alongside ready to depart for Portree, and the Cuillins of Skye forming a magnificent backdrop in the west.

Today's railway has 18 remaining miles to its terminus, delightfully snaking in and out of the rocky coastline over continuous curves, small bridges and causeways, and with increasingly dramatic landscapes culminating in fine views across the Inner Sound as the railway nears Kyle.

Plockton has always had only a single platform, but today it is the busiest intermediate station between Dingwall and Kyle, reflecting the attractive village's popularity. Seen in April 2017. *Merrill MacWilliam (from a photo by David Fasken)*

The first station after Strathcarron – on your left – is **Attadale** (one of six request stops on the Kyle line), just a short walk from the gardens of Attadale House, where the mild west-coast climate encourages a variety of conifers, rhododendrons and exotic plants to flourish in 20 acres of sheltered grounds. Beyond the gardens, the estate is today commercially run for stalking parties, but there are also self-catering cottages for visitors.

In another era, as Peter Tatlow notes in *The Dingwall & Skye Railway*, the diminutive railway halt opened in 1873 served little more than the big house which had been built in 1755, and was owned by Alexander Matheson of Ardross, 'but it was advertised to handle passenger, parcel, horse and goods traffic. The Highland Railway had to accept traffic where it could find it.'

Matheson, as we have seen, was one of the key driving forces behind the construction of the railway northwards from Inverness. From Attadale's diminutive platform – just one door on the train is opened – today's waiting passenger can spot metal 'chairs' (holding the rails in place on the wooden sleepers) marked 'LMS 1942', demonstrating that, in places, wear and tear on the line's infrastructure is very modest.

Beyond Attadale, an entirely new road was being constructed in 1969, when rock blasting led to two landslides which closed the railway for periods of up to 17 weeks. During the closure, the UK's only road and rail avalanche shelter was constructed at one of the most susceptible locations – and the line had to be shifted further seaward to provide sufficient space for the new A890 road at the foot of the rocky outcrops. Steel-meshed netting was also draped over the surrounding cliffs – a common sight across the rail network today, but most unusual in 1970. Roaring waterfalls are a distinctive feature

The old and the (relatively) new: the moulded metal columns of Plockton's distinctive station frame the 13.22 departure to Kyle on 5 April 2017. *David Fasken*

of this stretch, and, regrettably, rock falls are not uncommon, although it is generally the road, being closer to the rock face, which suffers more from the falling rocks.

A glance ahead through the window demonstrates just how twisting the alignment of the railway has become. For most of the way from Attadale to Stromeferry (as it is now spelt in the railway timetable), the train's speed is limited to just 25 mph, rising thereafter to a heady 30 mph towards Kyle. An even grander view draws the eye across Loch Carron to the village of the same name, with – on a clear day – the peak of Bad a' Chreamha (1,296 feet) prominent to the west of the village.

Continuing concerns about rock falls have led to discussions about the railway here being 'tramwayed' – that is, with the rail track set within the road, as far as possible from the adjacent cliffs – but this would involve special safety regulations. It has been suggested that this would require the railway to be restricted to specialist light-weight train units, such as the 'D-train' diesel-electric multiple-unit being converted from London Underground rolling stock by Vivarail, but commentators have noted that conventional trains travelling at 25 mph on the Welsh Highland Railway (the same speed as Kyle trains along Loch Carron) routinely share space with cyclists and pedestrians, on a stretch of tramwayed track controlled by traffic lights for rail and road vehicles.

If *only* light-weight trains were permitted on this stretch of the Kyle line – where the 1970 road 'improvements' have ever since caused problems for the railway – then charter trains, such as the *Royal Scotsman,* and freight trains, would be banned from the Kyle line for ever, a tragic waste of the line's capability as a safe and sustainable means of transport from Scotland's east to west coasts.

A detail of one of Plockton station's moulded metal columns, seen in April 2017. *Merrill MacWilliam (from a photo by David Spaven)*

At **Stromeferry** there is little sign of the station's former status as the terminus of the line, although today's single platform (on your right) is attractively laid out in gravel and the redundant second platform (on your left) has survived in good condition. There is woodland where railway sidings once served the Kishorn oil platform construction yard, helping to save the route from closure in 1974. We have to use our imagination to picture the timber train shed which once spanned both tracks and both platforms, but HA Vallance in *The Highland Railway* brings to life one of the most unusual incidents in the history of the railway:

The Skye line never enjoyed Sunday services. In all probability, lightness of traffic was the determining factor. On the other hand, the people of Wester Ross were evidently strict sabbatarians in the early days of the railway. Pendleton, in *Our Railways*, records a serious disturbance which occurred at Strome Ferry in 1883, when it was desired to run a Sunday fish special:

A remarkable scene was witnessed at Strome Ferry – on (Sunday) June 3rd, 1883. The people were determined at all hazards that others beside themselves should keep the Sabbath. The Railway Company proposed to send a load of fish by special train, so that the provender might be taken on by the limited mail (from Inverness). When the fishing boats came inshore to offload, the villagers mustered, armed with clubs and sticks. They menaced the crews, and prevented the landing of the fish. Not only the police, but the railway officials intervened; but the combined forces were overcome by the indignant coast-dwellers, who took possession of the pier and the station.

'Black 5' No. 45305 hauls a tourist charter train past Erbusaig on the final leg of the journey to Kyle on 23 April 2012. *Allan Beattie*

The crowd prayed and sang in the railway station and – actually remembered the Directors in the supplications – until midnight, when traffic was resumed. Ten of the men, found guilty of mobbing and rioting, were sent to prison for four months each. The riot was the subject of questions in the House of Commons, and Sir William Harcourt, then Home Secretary, replied that if the men had really expressed sincere regret he would consult with the judge with a view to securing a remission of the sentence. He did consult with his lordship; and on September 23rd the men were liberated from Calton Jail, Edinburgh.

When regular all-year Sunday passenger trains finally began operation in 2001, there was no controversy. But, in reaching their decision to extend the railway a further 10½ miles from Strome Ferry to Kyle of Lochalsh in the 1890s, the Directors of the Highland Railway had had to consider some powerful arguments: on the one hand, the competitive threat posed by the imminent arrival of the West Highland Railway at Fort William (in 1894) and its mooted extension to Mallaig and, on the other hand, the undoubted difficulty of construction through hard Torridonian sandstone most of the way to Kyle. However, the tough task undertaken from 1893 to 1897 by Victorian engineers and navvies – with not a few casualties in the process – has bequeathed the modern traveller a twisting, turning journey of changing vistas and scenic surprises.

The first section takes the railway along 'raised beaches' whose origins lie in the period between 6,000 and 3,000 BC, when melting ice sheets led to higher sea levels. Following removal of the huge

With the mountains of Skye in the distance, a Class 26 waits to leave Kyle with the late afternoon train to Inverness on 15 September 1973. The milk van at the front of the train will be detached at Dingwall. *Bill Roberton*

weight of ice, this section of land mass has been steadily rising, leaving these beaches literally 'high and dry'.

Among heavily forested coastal slopes, fringed with a riot of yellow gorse, and through deep cuttings blasted from solid rock (now lined by massive steel-mesh netting), comes the tiny, B-listed request stop at **Duncraig**. Built as a private halt to serve Alexander Matheson's Duncraig Castle – in turn one of the fruits of the vast fortunes made from Far East opium by the family business, Jardine Matheson – it became a naval hospital during World War Two and was subsequently converted into a domestic science college. It is currently undergoing restoration before opening as a luxury hotel in 2018. 'Duncraig Halt' was one of three Beeching-inspired station closures on the Kyle line in 1964, but it re-opened to the public just 12 years later.

Beyond Duncraig, the railway sweeps around the southern shore of **Plockton** Bay, with great views towards the village of the same name – now more of an picturesque sailing resort than a settlement of crofters and fishers.

The BBC TV series *Hamish MacBeth* was filmed at Plockton, and the local natural environment is now benefiting from the re-introduction of red squirrels in a lottery-funded project led by the Scottish Wildlife Trust and Trees for Life.

The B-listed station building – dating from Highland Railway days – is one of the few surviving large timber structure along the line, and vies with Duncraig for the status of the most attractive building on the Kyle line. Today it houses self-catering facilities which could not be handier for

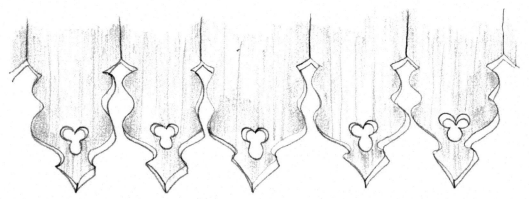

Victorian wood carving, still evident at Kyle station's main platform in April 2017. *Merrill MacWilliam (from a photo by David Spaven)*

the rail-based tourist, complemented (on your left) by a modern bunkhouse built in the style of a traditional railway signal box. Plockton is the busiest intermediate station between Dingwall and Kyle.

The line then plunges up and down steep gradients through **Duirinish** where, even if no passengers request a stop, trains are speed-restricted across the adjacent level crossing. Immediately beyond Duirinish (on your left) is the crofting settlement of Drumbuie, once controversially proposed as a site for oil platform construction on National Trust for Scotland lands.

The twists and turns continue round Erbusaig Bay and its distinctive causeway carrying the railway over the water, and soon the train begins to slow down on the final approach to the railway's terminus, with the road bridge linking the mainland and Skye usually visible to the south. The end of this special journey certainly lives up to all the promotional plaudits, with a deep cutting opening out into the terminus, and the single-track railway splitting into two tracks either side of the attractive, B-listed, timber-built station at **Kyle of Lochalsh**, jutting out towards Loch Alsh on the original Highland Railway pier with, weather permitting, the towering peaks of Skye looming beyond.

Kyle is by far the busiest station on the line. Of the 100,000 ScotRail passengers per year who travel west of Dingwall, no fewer than two-thirds arrive at or depart from the Kyle terminus. And Kyle is overwhelmingly the destination for charter train passengers. The village – with a resident population of fewer than 1,000 – can, of course, be a stepping stone for further explorations by road and sea, with Scottish Citylink coaches heading westwards across the Skye Bridge to Portree and Uig (for ferry services to Tarbert on Harris and Lochmaddy on North Uist), and eastwards to Kintail and Fort William.

Metal work dating back to 1897 still adorns Kyle station's main platform in April 2017. *Merrill MacWilliam (from a photo by David Spaven)*

There is plenty to interest the rail traveller in and around the impressive station building: within the building are a restaurant, a shop and snack bar, and a museum, the last two run by the Friends of the Kyle Line group, as is the self-catering accommodation in the former signal box just north-east of the station. Above the signal box accommodation there is a model rail lay-out which you can visit by obtaining a key from the station. There is also the added attraction of a panoramic view towards the station and pier.

A trip to Kyle has all the ingredients for a memorable experience. However, unlike Michael Palin in 1980, on one of his early TV *Great Railway Journeys* – from London to Kyle – you won't be able to round off your trip by (at least, legally) carrying away a large station name board!

# CHAPTER FIVE

# Selected features

**Inverness** – Inverness & Aberdeen Junction Railway 1858 commemorative plaque; Frank Spaven memorial seat on Platform 2; original Highland Railway Lochgorm Works building in the track 'triangle' beyond the station

**Clachnaharry** – B-listed canal swing bridge and signal box (and nearby lineside view from the Clachnaharry Inn beer garden)

**Beauly** – Britain's smallest station (only one door on the train is opened)

**Conon Bridge** – B-listed viaduct over the River Conon

**Dingwall** – B-listed station; The Mallard bistro bar and Tina's Tearoom (www.tinastearoom.com/) on the station platform; B-listed Station Road warehouse

**Garve** – original stone-built Highland Railway station building and metal footbridge

**Achnasheen** – original stone-built Highland Railway station building and metal footbridge

**Achnashellach** – stepping-off point for the hike through the Coulin Pass to Torridon

**Strathcarron** – original stone-built Highland Railway station building and metal footbridge

**Attadale** – station adjacent to Attadale Gardens' conifers, rhododendrons and an artist's garden designed to frame the views of the surrounding hills (https://www.attadalegardens.com/)

**Duncraig** – B-listed station

**Plockton** – B-listed station: self-catering accommodation in station building (http://www.plocktonstation.co.uk/)

**Kyle of Lochalsh** – B-listed station and pier; restaurant in station building (http://www.watersideseafoodrestaurant.co.uk); shop and snack bar in station building (http://www.kylerailway.co.uk/kyle-line-shop-and-snack-bar/); museum in station building (http://www.kylerailway.co.uk/kyle-line-museum/); self-catering accommodation and model railway in signal box (http://www.kylerailway.co.uk/signal-box-holiday-apartment/)